DESIGN BY DESIRE

A Novel Of Charles Rennie Mackintosh

by

GD McNutt

For Alice

CONTENTS

FOREWORD

Charles Rennie Mackintosh (1868-1928) can go down in history as Scotland's greatest ever architect. He was also a prolific and underrated artist. Mackintosh was a creative genius far in advance of his time and it is this precociousness that, paradoxically, explains his tragedy .... a tragedy that saw him die miserable, penniless and in total obscurity.

Mackintosh was so far ahead of his time that he came to be rejected by the stuffy late Victorian and early Edwardian Establishment. His great masterpiece, The Glasgow School Of Art, so disconcerted the narrow-minded old patricians of the day that, after the completion of its first phase in 1899, he was never offered another serious commission.

Consequently, he became marginalised, a lost figure who wandered somewhat aimlessly until his death in 1928 after being forced out of Glasgow in 1914. Yet his architecture and his unique interiors remain fresh and alive today and look as though they may have been designed for a modern construction.

Some commentators have referred to this ostracising of Mackintosh from the mainstream and the subsequent waste of his talents as "The Mackintosh Myth". But what is so mythical about it?
Here was a man worshipped in Europe for his artistic vision yet shunned in his own country for what the Wee Grey Men no doubt regarded as his impetuousness. Effectively, they destroyed him.

This brutal destruction of the maverick genius by a staid, conservative and ultimately frightened Establishment has become repetitive and thematic in our society ... dating even back to the savage days when ignorant "clergymen" used to burn "witches". But a suspicious society's brutal destruction or suppression of an original and free spirit is also the stuff of great drama and the Mackintosh story deserves to be told.

Vincent Van Gough, a contemporary of Mackintosh, has been eulogised to saturation point after suffering a tortured life during which his talents and achievements were never recognised. It would be pointless here to suggest that Mackintosh suffered in the same way as Van Gough, but certainly there are parallels.

The Mackintosh story deserves to be told and any story of Charles Rennie Mackintosh must also be the story of his beloved wife Margaret Macdonald, a great artist and designer in her own right.
Yet this book is not a biography, and nor is it intended as a mere chronicle of linear events. Though I have taken the liberty of employing some slight embellishments, nor can this book be called a work of fiction.

Perhaps it might serve to call this a work of "faction", a most regrettable term. Recorded details of the lives of Mackintosh, Macdonald, their inner circle and other members of this illustrious cast are less than sketchy. I have endeavoured to colour them in a little. Consider then, that events in the story offered here may or may not have actually happened. But somehow I feel they must have.

(GD McNutt, Aberdeen, Summer 2017)

PROLOGUE

(Part One). Blackbirds

He awoke from a bad dream in which children choked to death in a burning chateau to find himself once again in the dingy surroundings of a bedroom that he hated. He hated even the bed that he lay in, but not so much from its ungainly design as for the fact that his slumber was so disturbed and intermittent these days that it had been a long time since he had enjoyed what might be termed a proper sleep. The pocket watch on the ugly bedside table beside him told him it was 10.30am.

So he had overslept again, but, he reflected, why use a word like "overslept" when he had nothing whatever to get up for. He sensed that there was no one else in the house with perhaps the possible exception of the morning chambermaid who, having long since completed her chores, might be having tea and cake in the cavernous stone-walled kitchen. His muscles ached and his head and eyes felt heavy and he considered closing them again and sleeping at least until noon. But he knew he wouldn't do it. He had to get out of that horrible bed.

As soon as he threw back the heavy quilt and swung his legs over the mattress to assume a sitting position, the pain in his throat knifed through his larynx and chest. The big ugly radium collar that he had been ordered to wear at all times by Doctor Henderson lay discarded on the hideous display table on the other side of the room. He would not put it on until he had to go down. He had been treating his tongue cancer not so much with the dreadful steel –and- rubber collar that made him feel like a shackled slave as with frequent nips from the silver flask of brandy for which he now reached. The ugly bedside table's drawer was stiff and he hardly had the strength to pull it open. The flask was engraved. "To My Darling Toshie From Your Devoted Margaret. No Border Could Ever Keep Us Apart"

1

Well, it was true, but he had been away from her too long. Now that he was back in London perhaps they could set about organising another exhibition. Certainly their London patron Doctor Hoffman seemed to be of the opinion that they now had enough of a following. If only it weren't for tis damned illness that left him so infernally listless all the time and damn-near half-drunk with the brandy that was all that seemed to ease the pain of it.

He forced himself to wash and dress and decided to go down to sit in the garden for a while. If there was nobody about, he needn't wear the blasted collar. Perhaps in the afternoon he would feel well enough to go and visit Margaret at the studio. He had no thought of breakfast, or even coffee. Swallowing was a torture so he had developed a technique of not having to actually swallow the brandy as much as pour it straight down his swollen throat.

It was early April now, reminding him that in just two months he would be sixty years old. Spring had always been his favourite season and he would sit in the garden no matter what the weather was like. On this particular London mid-morning in the year of nineteen-hundred-and-twenty-eight the weather was bright and cold. He liked it that way. It somehow reminded him of Vienna. Glorious Vienna, where he had spent his halcyon days.

He sat in his bath chair under the spreading plane tree near the ancient shed with the broken gutters. He put down his neglected copy of Homer, having been distracted by something that interested him far more than Greek Mythology. It was two blackbirds building a nest, but he saw that they weren't doing it properly. That is to say that, although the business of perfect nest-building had been hot-wired into the birds' DNA over eons, he saw that they were unaware of the precariousness of the nest's position. The birds were building where in the event of rain the main flow of the old shed's broken gutter would swamp the nest and drown the hatchlings.

He got up out of his bath chair, slowly, painfully, with some vague notion of redirecting the gutter. He knew that if he moved the nest the blackbirds would abandon it, but perhaps starting over again elsewhere might at least save their offspring. Two steps from the chair he was suddenly gripped by a violent and paralysing seizure so intense that he thought someone must have whacked him over the head from behind using some heavy object. He fell to his knees on the slabbed patio, unable to catch his breath, suffocating now like the most chronic asthmatic , his shoulders convulsing as he began to spew out great gobs of red-black sticky blood that stained the base of a marble sundial. Choking to death, he tried to cry out for help but no sound emitted from his cancer-ridden throat.

He fell forward on to stones and rolled a half-turn, crashing into an ornate occasional table on which had been placed a large vase full of tulips. A terrible hoarse croaking now begin to come out of his throat along with the shaded blood that when he saw it did not alarm him but made him think only of The Odyssey's wine-dark sea.

The vase of tulips hit the stone patio and shattered with a loud smash and only then did he hear a commotion in the house as the chamber maid came running from the kitchen. He rolled again, on to his back this time, and looked up gratefully at a cobalt blue sky in which only a few wisps of cirrrhus glided like swans in a millpond. Just before consciousness faded, he smiled broadly as he caught a final glimpse of the two blackbirds winging away.

PROLOGUE (Part Two)

The Woman In The Conservatory

Wilbur Shriver did not much care for hot sunny days but didn't have the gumption to ask himself what he was doing in the South of France in the month of July.

It was simply the Done Thing, the grand tour of Europe that all wealthy Americans who aspired to any sort of social standing simply had to experience in order that it could be worn as some kind of badge of acceptance to that exclusive club on the other side of the Atlantic known, pejoratively or otherwise, as the Hampton WASPS.

Whether or not these tourists actually enjoyed themselves was completely irrelevant. Nor did it matter in the least to Wilbur Shriver, and even less so to his belligerent wife Mabel , that the acronym stood for White Anglo-Saxon Protestant when Wilbur and his spouse could be more accurately described, not as WASPS, but FLYs (Fat Loquacious Yid).

Loquacious, yes, but certainly not lingual, and it was this unfortunate state of affairs that led to the small commotion in the lobby of the Hotel Du Commerce which, despite its name evoking images of overweight salesmen in threadbare suits and carrying cheap suitcases, was one of the more salubrious establishments in the pretty coastal town of Port Vendres.

"Speak English can't ya?" Wilbur exhorted a suddenly alarmed-looking concierge, a small thin fellow sporting a Dali-esque moustache who, in the manner so characteristic of Frenchmen at home forced to deal with unpleasant foreigners, was pretending not to understand them.

"Air- conditioning," interjected Mabel Shriver, fanning herself belligerently with some kind of tourist pamphlet. "We need a room where the air-conditioning actually works, not like in that last hotel in Madrid. We're from Wisconsin. Know where that is, huh? Not used to this Goddamn heat."

The eyes of the concierge widened even more, as if he could not quite believe the sheer size of Mabel's floral-patterned dress or how she managed to bear the weight of the various harvests of plastic fruit arranged around her wide straw hat.

"Honest to God, Wilbur, if he shrugs his shoulders like that one more time I swear I'll sit on his neck."
She said this not as a quiet aside to her sweating husband but in a loud yankee scraik which no one in the environs of the hotel reception could have failed to hear, including, of course, the now slightly terrified concierge.

"Surely there must be somebody around here who speaks English."

Wilbur, who generally regarded sarcasm to be right up there in the highest echelons of humour, piped up in support of his wife. "Now, now Mabel, take it easy. Why should there be anyone at all around here who speaks English? We are in the South of France after all."

"Yeah" she replied to Wilbur while continuing to stare at the concierge. "A little too far south if you ask me. This place looks more like the back of beyond."

In truth, the concierge was actually somewhat more rattled by this question of air-conditioning than with the presence of the two uncouth Americans. The Hotel Du Commerce had never installed it . . . . had never seen the need. All rooms benefited from the cooling effects of numerous large ceiling fans and the pleasant breeze carrying in off the Mediterranean. French doors in every room at the front of the hotel led out to spacious balconies and a sea view. This arrangement had kept patrons returning to the Hotel Du Commerce over the fifty years since it had first opened its doors in 1879. The only other half-decent hotel in town, the Grenache, had, the concierge knew, installed the Williams system only the previous year, in 1928, and it had kept on breaking down. Something to do with Corsican electricians. Perhaps the Shrivers might be happier at the Grenache but he remained keen to help them. He had been pretending not to fully understand them until he gave himself enough time to come up with the right strategy regarding their request. Also, he was looking for a promotion and did not want to lose them. Imbecilic philistines they they were. Dollars was his favourite English word. He came out through the flap from behind his desk and bowed theatrically in front of them.

"English yes," he said. "Please Madame, follow me."

Well, he certainly walked like a concierge, thought Mabel, as she and Wilbur followed the Frenchman through what seemed like a tunnel of aspidistras. Almost militarily and just a little bit effeminate.

He stopped at the door of a large conservatory and, theatrically again, like a character in a Hollywood Silent Comedy Film, peered through the algaed glass.

"Madam" he looked at Mabel and nodded towards the conservatory's interior. "This ladee, Mrs Mackintosh, parlez Anglaise. Her husband, I theenk he was an artist."

Mabel Shriver, suspicious and still much put out, looked through the glass. But just then he frown gradually changed to a smile and,

6

gingerly, she turned the door handle as if trying not to startle the person inside. Wilbur followed her in.

"Pardon me, mam," Mabel's tone had become almost reverent. "The concierge says you are English. We need someone who speaks the language a little better than he does..... I wonder if you'd mind. We are the Shrivers, mam, Wilbur and Mabel, from Green Bay, Wisconsin, a lovely spot on the south shore of Lake Michigan, a little cold in winter, of course, perhaps you know it? The little man at reception said you husband was famous. Should I have heard of him?."

Wilbur Shiver, somewhat perplexed by this last utterance of his wife whom he felt was too often given to flights of fancy, quickly interjected.

"He did not say famous. He said he was an artist, that's all. Plenty of artists in France. Only famous Mackintosh I've heard of is that rubberised cloth guy. That who you are?"

The woman in the conservatory, who had never ceased to be amazed by the presumptuousness, or perhaps it was desperation, of Americans who wanted one to have visited or to be familiar with the tiny backwater in the middle of the vast continent from where they came, smiled a little to herself.

Perhaps it was the comedy of their appearance, perhaps their near-childish earnestness, but she had already made up her mind to be kind to these people. How could it hurt her? And if they persisted, she could always let them down a little less gently later on.

At the age of 64 Margaret Macdonald, or Madam Mackintosh as she was known in the hotel and to certain villagers in the wider community of Port Vendres, was still a striking- looking woman, tall and slim with thick auburn hair, immaculately dressed and exuding an other-wordly air of elegance.

But her facial beauty had been tarnished by her years of fighting the endometriosis that had struck her in her mid-thirties and which and which put the hope of ever bearing a child completely out of the question. Still, today she was having one of her good days and was of a disposition to receive these interlopers, perhaps even desirous of a little company.

"English, my dear," she extended a bejewelled hand to the Shriver woman. "Well, it is true that I was born there but by blood I am a Scot. And my dear late husband was certainly never famous . . . .at least not in his own country. Infamous, perhaps. He was an artist, you know, and an architect of great sensitivity and originality. I assisted him in many of his projects. We used to call it design by desire."

Delighted by the raciness of this phrase, and uttered as it was by such a statuesque and elegant woman, Mabel pressed home her advantage.

"Oh my, I just knew you had to be somebody," she gushed. "Wilbur and me went to the Louvre but I got one of my headaches. There was just too much. I just couldn't take it all in. Would I have seen any of your husband's work? What kind paintings did he do?"

Margaret indicated a small-framed watercolour propped up on a garden chair opposite the one she had been sitting in. It was one of Mackintosh's studies of the village of Coulliore, a few miles from Port Vendres, and she had been cleaning it. Now she lifted the painting and held it so that the bright sunshine streaming in through the conservatory roof lit it up from behind.

"This is one of Toshie's," she said, though staring off into the middle distance, she was no longer addressing the Shrivers. "But it is owned by the hotel now. He sold it to them. We were quite poor. It is beautiful, don't you think? I loved everything he did, you know... everything. And I never hated him for giving up because, you know, there was really nothing he could have done about it. It was the war, you see."

Her sudden change in demeanour seemed to alarm the Shriver woman, who quickly lost interest in viewing the watercolour and instead took a few steps backwards. But Margaret continued as if in a trance, her tone becoming more and more strident.

"Yes, Charles was a truly great man, yet how modest in his greatness. He used to say that he was nothing without me, that I was threequarters of all his architectural efforts and that I had genius, whereas he himself had only talent. But how wrong he was, how wrong. It was just the opposite, my dear. And look what they did to him. They destroyed him. They excluded him. They even arrested him. They ostracised him and called him superficial. Such a waste, my dear, such a terrible, tragic waste . . "

Margaret sat back down in her raffia chair and hugged the watercolour to her breast. Mabel Shriver was now experiencing mild fear. Wilbur was already pointing back the way they had come in. He took his wife by the arm.

"Thank you, ma'am. We won't be bothering you anymore. Come on, Mabel."

The Americans left the conservatory a lot faster than they had entered it, leaving a woman who now sat with her long legs pulled up around her, as if in some attempt at self- protection, a woman who began to mutter to herself while staring at the painting she held with a terrified face. When she heard the exit door open as the Shrivers reached it, she leapt up and called after them.

"But you didn't tell me what you wanted. How can I help you?"

But the Americans had gone, leaving her alone once more among the pungent flora. She looked at the painting again, repeating over

and over, this time to the painting itself, "How can I help you?....
How can I help you?

And then, setting the painting back in the chair, she removed her clips to let her long, auburn-grey hair cascade down her back, releasing the top four buttons of her linen tunic and kicking off her sandals. She picked up the painting again and once more clutched it to her breast. And then she began to dance with it, gliding around the conservatory, slowly at first in a steady waltz, but then faster and faster until her long hair began to swirl through the flowers that drooped as she held the painting aloft again in her crazy choreography of grief and regret.

CHAPTER ONE

The Four

She was holding the painting aloft in a bid to defeat the gloom of the depressing common room in the old Glasgow College Of Art, so as to give her three companions the clearest possible opportunity to interpret the essence of what she was trying to convey. It displayed the Beardsleyesque image of one of her thin, androgynous women, an elongated figure, its swirling hair entangled with the stems of the enormous cabbage roses that featured, almost randomly, in most of her creations. The women in the paintings were so like herself, yet she would have strongly denied any suggestion that she was producing self-portraits.

She was twenty-seven years old now, and still beautiful, but perhaps possessed of a mild sense of panic that, as she rapidly approached the milestone age of thirty, she was destined to remain a forever obscure dot on the Art Nouveau landscape of the burgeoning new world of interior design that was spreading throughout Europe. It was true that she would soon have her own studio, at 128 Hope Street, which she would run in partnership with her younger sister. Their designs were already inspired by Celtic imagery and folklore and created through the mediums of metalwork, embroidery and textiles, as well as watercolour. But Glasgow was such an unfashionable backwater and she knew that she would have to exhibit abroad.

She was showing her painting to three companions yet hoped it would be appraised by only one of them, the one on whom she was pinning her hopes, the one she felt possessed the power to give them all wings. She did not care if, like Icarus, they flew too near to the sun. She only wanted to have her chance.

To some, her works,   symbolic as they were of the "New Woman" spirit of the times, were mildly seditious, a somehow affront to an Empire created by testosterone and chicanery. To others, they were merely grotesque and ghostly so that, depending on which side of the fence one reclined, the quartet of bright young things in the dingy old common room would be known with no little reverence as The Four, or, with an equal amount of ridicule , as The Spook School.

The young man to whom Margaret Macdonald was directing most of her attention was already something of an acknowledged prodigy and did not, yet at least, fully share her conviction that the only way up was out of grim Clydeside. It was no secret that the 25-year-old Charles Rennie Mackintosh, or simply Tosh as she called him, though at first he had been shocked by this taking of liberties, was being fast-tracked at Honeyman and Keppie, the rising firm of architects which had just won the commission for the new Glasgow Herald building, which Mackintosh himself would design.

Certainly, this young man looked as handsome as his prospects . . . the big, noble Highland head crowned by a generous mop of curly black hair, the soft dark-brown eyes, the sparkle in which seemed to be accentuated by a generous nose under which reclined the moustache of a cavalier. That he was not the tallest of men hardly seemed to matter to the bevy of young women drawn to him. But perhaps more of a testament to his general attractiveness was the fact that neither did they care about his club foot or that he walked with a slight limp. It was the result of having a contracted sinew in his left foot but It seemed only to add to the mystique of the man.

Margaret's other two companions, the couple who made up The Four, rose from their chairs to get a closer look at her work. Her sister Frances and Frances's cohort Herbert MacNair, were already practically an item. The similarity between these four people was remarkable, with the 20-year-old Frances a slightly shorter version of her sister, so that they were often taken to be twins. MacNair was the same age as Mackintosh and seemed to be merely a taller version.

He also worked at Honeyman and Keppie, where the two had become firm friends.

Mackintosh gently took the painting from Margaret. He found that he liked standing close to her. As well as forming their own artistic cabal, The Four were also members of a group of young intellectuals who called themselves The Immortals, some of whom, disgusted by Victorian hypocrisy, advocated social revolution and even free love. As a result, when in no other company The Four spoke unencumbered by any social cenorship.

Mackintosh smiled at the work he now held. "This is wonderful, Margaret. We really must see about you and Frances getting your own exhibition. Perhaps headmaster Newbery would allow one here in the school."

"Too limited," said MacNair. "It would have to be in the International Exhibition Hall in Kelvingrove Park, or maybe in some castle or palace, to give it any gravitas. They need to be taken seriously."

Margaret flushed with pleasure but restrained her imagination. "My dear boys," she said, "how I love the spirit of you optimism. But what chance have obscure students of an exhibition when Glasgow turns away the masters. I couldn't get hanged in Gordon's tea room."

MacNair guffawed. "Now that really would have the dowagers choking on their sodie scones. I thought they hanged people at Glasgow Cross."

"Paintings are hung, people are hanged," said Frances.

But MacNair, devil's advocate now, couldn't stop himself. He loved the fact that Frances was five years his junior and would often grab any opportunity to tease or titillate.

"Oh really, my dear," he said. "Well, that's not what I hear about yon wee Frenchman Toulouse-Lautrec. They say that he hung well enough, like a stallion if you will, and that the Paris whores have the bruises to prove it."

"Herbert, you've a mouth like a midden," said Frances, but she was really more pleased than ruffled.

In mentioning Toulouse-Lautrec, MacNair knew he had entered a small corner of Mackintosh's own territory. The Mackintosh club foot.

13

The Frenchman whose legs did not grow beyond childhood, so that he had a man's torso on legs of a ten-year-old boy. But Mackintosh had been amused by the exchange between his friend and Frances.

"It would seem that the diminutive French monsieur is both hung and hanged," laughed Mackintosh. "Those posters of his are turning the heads of even the most
respectable Parisian patriarchs. What poor Parisian wife is not now a widow to the Moulin Rouge? What power the wee man wields in his paintbrush. These pictorial posters of his are the coming thing. We should maybe pay them some attention."

Just then there came a rapping on the pane of the common-room door and the somewhat disgruntled face of a plain young woman could be seen behind the glass, peering in. Mackintosh immediately saw that it was Jessie Keppie, the daughter of his employer. The talk of the steamie was that Jessie and Charles were being groomed to one day become husband and wife and Jessie's presence now presented the young architect with a delicate situation. In this, the infancy of his career, he needed his job with the firm, not to mention John Keppie's support and contacts. Marrying Jessie would be a smart move. If only he weren't already in love with Margaret.

The sight of Jessie's head through the glass made Margaret impish. "I say, Tosh, I believe you are being summoned."

Mackintosh was annoyed but didn't show it. "Blast, I completely forgot all about it. I promised Jessie she could accompany me to Annan's today for the portrait. She's sure to want to take the blasted picture herself."

Margaret still teased. "A portrait of the happy couple, eh Tosh? Can we expect the Banns to be posted soon?"

This elicited a faint betrayal of annoyance. "Happy couple my eye," he said. "I am having my photograph taken to promote myself and my vocation. Jessie doesn't come into it, even if she thinks otherwise. Christ, I have twenty minutes to get home and change."

The classroom door opened followed by the swift and businesslike entrance of a young woman wearing a somewhat disgruntled expression. It was the year of Our Lord Eighteen Hundred and Ninety Three and the month was April, but the woman was still dressed for winter, her fur coat wrapped tightly around her under a warm slouch hat. Jessie Keppie was also part of The Immortals, though there were some members who suspected that her heart wasn't fully in it. It was, of course, one way of getting to socialise with Charles Rennie Mackintosh. She nursed her wrath, peeved that Mackintosh had not called for her at the appointed minute but reluctant to display herself to the others as any kind of harridan. She scarcely paused to greet the others before homing in on the subject of her mission.

"Charles, for heaven's sake do you know what time it is? Don't answer that, just come with me right away. It seems that everyone from the Prime Minister to the postmaster is having their picture taken and Annan is a busy man."

Mackintosh decided the best way to avoid losing any more face in front of the other three members of the four was to play this one for laughs. "My dear Jessie, what would I do without you? But for the price Annan is charging he can wait for me a few more minutes. I'll need to go and change."

He turned to the others, anxious now only to get away from Margaret while Jessie was in the process of chiding him. He bowed theatrically.

"Until we meet again, my friends, posterity, if not posters, awaits. They say that the camera does not lie and I am truly dishevelled."

He offered Jessie his arm, again theatrically, and they left the classroom. Margaret watched them go, her impish smile not fading. He had offered Jessie his arm, but Margaret knew that his semi-comedic performance had been for her benefit and that he had been as chivalrous as the situation would allow. Frances and Herbert laughed at some irreverent joke of his made at Jessie's expense but to Margaret their laughter was coming from far away. Her expression was benign, contented, expectant even, and seemed to mirror almost exactly the one on the face of the woman she had created, the subject of the painting she had been holding out to Mackintosh.

15

CHAPTER TWO

Cravat and Ties

He stood in front of the cheval mirror in his bedroom at his parents'
house in Parson Street, where he still lived, preparing himself for his
photographic portrait. He reckoned he could get to Annan's in
Sauchiehall Street in fifteen minutes but, with Jessie in tow, the cab
would be expensive and he seemed always these days to be skint.
His resolve wavered a little as he took in his full reflection. He was
not dressed as might be expected of a young architect of the period.
There was no stiff collar, sober suit or slicked-down hair. Instead, he
wore a loose collar on to which he had tied a large, red, silk cravat,
gathered up in a big mock-careless bow. His suit was light-grey wool
and casual, his white shirt worn open at the top three buttons neck
underneath the ostentatious neckwear. His rich, dark hair was
mercifully free of any oil or water. His full moustache, not quite
handlebar, perfectly completed the image of a dashing cavalier. Here
was a young man with no interest in presenting himself as a
provincial architect, or indeed as any kind of a professional
businessman. Here was a young man who clearly wanted to be
regarded as an artist. His courage returned. Damn them all, he
thought, this is how I am going to be. I've had it with all their pomp
and stuffiness.

The knock on his bedroom door was undeniably Jessie's. He had
come to know that knock. The voice in the hall was strident.

"Charles. For heaven's sake, you really must come now or the
game won't be worth the candle."

"Christ, Jessie, he shouted back to her. "I hope Annan can afford
something better than candles. He should do for the money I'm
paying."

He opened the door and when she came into the room he again
bowed theatrically, before stepping back to display himself to her in

all his Bohemian finery. But Jessie's plain face fell. She succeeded in maintaining her decorum but was obviously struggling to restrain her inner fury.

"Well, Charles" she spluttered. "I was under the impression we were going out to have your professional portrait done, not driving up to the loch for a cream tea picnic. Well, it's too late now. By the time you change your clothes again and get us to Sauchiehall Street Annan will have shut up shop. We'll just have to make another appointment that's all. And it'll be dearer next time. Really, Charles, what were you thinking?"
This outburst left him more puzzled than annoyed and again he wondered about Jessie. The woman was not completely soulless. She was, after all, a member of The Immortals and an award-winning designer in her own right.

Yet she remained enslaved by convention. He reflected, with some bitterness, that she was probably considering the sensitivities of her brother rather than those of Mackintosh himself when she had obviously decided what Mackintosh should be wearing for his portrait. John Keppie would be horrified to see his firm advertised or represented by a dilettante. He swallowed his annoyance. He had no wish to be harsh. He would try to explain it to her.

"What was I thinking of, Jessie? If only you knew, and if I took the time to tell you then Annan really would be shut --- for the weekend. I was thinking, Jessie, of cathedrals that don't frighten the weans, of libraries where people can sit and read unoppressed by heat or cold, of houses where families can commune without having to make appointments or trip over one another, of public buildings where people can work without feeling they are in some hostile warehouse with a millstone around their necks. In short, Jessie, I was thinking of architecture for human beings in all their complexity and not merely soulless edifices of practical construction."
She was caught in the dilemma of her love for him and her hopes for his professional future. A wave of tenderness swept over her and

17

she wanted to go to him. It vexed her sorely that he never displayed any physical affection toward her these days. The wave of tenderness suddenly washed up on rocks of bitter resentment.

"Charles, there is no need to take that tone," she said. "My only concern is for your future .... for our future. Just how many commissions do you think you are going to get if you present yourself as some artistic dreamer with one foot on the left bank of the River Sienne. People want respectability. Honestly, this is what comes of spending too much time with those Macdonald sisters and that daft big MacNair. And don't think I don't see the way that Margaret looks at you. But you mind me, Charles, you'll never get anywhere mixing with that lot. My brother has high hopes for you. It's about time you started living up to them."

Her mention of the firm quickly sobered the mood of gaiety he had hitherto been enjoying. He knew he couldn't afford to blow his chance. He was a working-class boy from a family of twelve brought up on the breadline of the father's policeman wages.

"I can assure you Jessie that whatever hopes John has for me I am grateful for. But it just might be that John and me have differing notions about what architecture should be. To him, it is a job. To me, it is the supreme discipline because it alone uniquely brings all the arts together. To understand my work you have to see it as a complete unit rather than as individual components. I want to connect people with my buildings, both functionally and spiritually."

"And yet you are no clergyman," she scoffed.

"I don't have to be, Jessie. I believe that I can make a building embrace the human soul and that this can be achieved through the careful balancing of opposites . . . modernity with tradition, masculine with feminine, light with shade, sensuality with frigidity. The Bhuddists live by it, don't you know. And, after all, Bhuddism is the religion of the most densely-populated country in the world and the first to be civilised. If I can do that here then I will have achieved something. It not just a job to me, Jessie, but a vocation. Your brother is helping me at the beginning of what I perceive will be a long and difficult road but if you cannot see what I am pursuing then I fear there is little hope for us."

18

Stricken by those last few words of his, Jessie turned on her heel and left the room. She would never forsake him, but in the sadness of her future years she would often reflect on that moment and of those words which had cut her so much on the day of the appointment for the portrait. She had thought it was going to be a happy day and had so much looked forward to it. Six years hence, when Mackintosh will break off their engagement leaving her devastated and depressed, she will remember this day. The loss of him will destroy her. She will never speak his name again and will die an old and embittered maid.

Alone in his bedroom at his parents' house once more, Mackintosh took a deep breath and made the final adjustments to his appearance. He felt sure that, despite the gravity of his words, Jessie would never do anything to jeopardise his position with the firm. He decided to treat himself to a cab in order to keep his appointment with Annan and as he left the house there was a certain lightness in his step. He felt himself to be starting out on the road to his destiny.

CHAPTER THREE:

Invitations and Exhibitions

If Charles Rennie Mackintosh had started on the road to his destiny then he was as yet a hitch-hiker. For the next eighteen months the firm kept him hard at it, yet nothing turned up to fully stimulate his imagination or tempt his talent. He took solace in his private design work and in summer holidays spent sketching in the English Cotswolds, from where he wrote to both Margaret and Jessie.

But then in December of 1894 a letter addressed to him arrived at the offices of Honeyman and Keppie at 140 Bath Street. Ordinarily, Mackintosh took nothing to do with the morning mail, which was all left to Mary the secretary. He had always had some difficulty with reading and writing, a source of no little embarrassment since the condition of dyslexia was not recognised in his time. Here was a man who drew exquisite blueprints and who even invented his own typeface, yet struggled to read any book. He was not religious, yet God's irony was not lost on him.

Anything of import in the morning post would be brought to his attention either by Mary or by Keppie himself, but on this day one envelope stood out from the others by dint of having his name on it and by bearing the seal of the Prussian Ministry of Public Works in Berlin. He opened it to see that while written on official notepaper, the letter had not been typed but was three pages of the author's longhand and couched in a friendly and informal style. He almost choked on his coffee when he saw that it was signed Hermann Muthesius. He knew that Muthesius was a leading patron of the decorative arts in the new Germany, a powerful emerging nation in the middle of Europe that had so recently been unified by the political genius of Otto Von Bismarck. He knew that Muthesius was a writer, publisher and the creative director of Corazon, one of the leading European design houses with centres in Munich and Vienna.

The man was also assistant to the Reichstag architect Paul Wallot. What he didn't know was why such a distinguished illuminary was writing to him.

He read laboriously. Muthesius wrote that, having just returned from Tokyo, where he was working as architect to a German construction company, he had been struck by the obvious Japanese influence in the designs of Mackintosh so far published in the trade magazines. He said that he would soon be relocating to London where he would be cultural attaché to the German Embassy, with a remit to study British technical achievements. He would be writing a book about it. He would like to include Mackintosh and his work on the Glasgow Herald building in the book. He would be coming to Britain in January, as a kind of scouting visit, and his intention was to visit Scotland, where he very much hoped to meet Herr Mackintosh and other leading exponents of the Glasgow Style.

As Mackintosh walked through a light snowfall that evening on his way to meet the others at the old School of Art, he began to compose his reply to this Teutonic cultural giant. He would have to get it right. This could be his big chance, the one he had been waiting for. European exposure, Teutonic or otherwise, might just be the making of him. But he also knew he must learn to walk before he could run. His only high-profile commission, passed to him somewhat reluctantly by Keppie, since the Herald building in Mitchell Street Lane was the Queen Margaret Medical College, for which he had been commended. He felt that Glasgow could not contain him, but that he still had much to achieve there. One thing about the Muthesius letter. It had instilled in him a new sense of hope and had propelled him out of his limbo. He felt happier than he had for some months. There were two wine merchants' shops on his way up from Bath Street to the old corporation buildings in Sauchiehall Street and he went into the first one of them.

"It doesn't seem quite right to be drinking Champagne out of stoorie old teacups," said Herbert MacNair, "but considering where we are I'll try to grin and bear it. How on earth can you afford to buy this stuff, Tosh?"

There had already been a mild air of excitement in the old common room before Mackintosh had walked in and produced his bottle. The approach of Christmas was generally a fecund period for the two Macdonald sisters but this December they had been even more inspired by the prospect of the School of Art Club Exhibition, which was to be held in January and in which their work was to feature prominently.

Margaret looked intently at Mackintosh as he poured her more Champagne. She felt that his generous spirit was manifest in his material extravagance and it was one of the traits of his that she found so endearing. But it also worried her a little. She had known him to "waste" money on wine when he needed to buy bread.

"So what's the occasion, Tosh?" asked Frances. "Is it just the festive season, or has Keppie handed you a diamond. Mind you, you've never needed an excuse of any kind to imbibe."

Mackintosh picked up the banter. "isn't she superb?" he said to the other two. "The epitomy of all light and joy. A veritable angel who sees hope in mediocrity and promise in the prosaic."

Frances blushed and Margaret laughed.

"But yes my dear," Mackintosh continued with his gentle mocking. "I see that high intelligence complements your ephemeral beauty. It has enabled you to probe my secret. Indeed this is an occasion, an occasion above and beyond the usual festive one, and we are gathered here to celebrate."

He produced the Muthesius letter and spread it out on the nearest desk for any or all to examine.

MacNair was in the right mood to prolong the banter. "It says here he will have a remit to study British technical achievements," he scoffed. "Spy on them, more like. D'ye not know that the Germans are currently in the process of building a navy with which they hope to match or outstrip our own. And them a land-locked country. Still, I'm impressed, Charles. But what does he want with you? You're hardly elevated enough for him to want to recruit as a Fifth Columnist."

Mackintosh persisted in his tone of mock indignation. "Ever the cynic, eh Herbie? But let me assure you that this man is not

22

interested in barbaric warmongering. He is an artist himself. The Herald building in Mitchell Street, that's what he wants with me. My first big job for the firm. He wants to include photographs of it in his posh new outrageously expensive coffee-table classic DIE ENGLISCHE BANKUNST Der GEGENWART, which roughly translates to Freestyle Architecture In Britain. He says that despite its clever details, the Scottish plainness of my work stands out among its English contemporaries. Ahem, could be he lost something in the translation there."

Margaret always defended him. "Plainness, indeed. What a cheek, Tosh. No one could ever describe your work as plain. I'd like to meet this man and give him my own measured opinion of HIS work."

He delightedly called her bluff. "By all means Margaret. I will be happy to introduce you. Herr Muthesius. He arrives in Glasgow on January 25th and has asked to meet me the following day. He WANTS me to introduce him to other Glasgow Stylists and, of course, above all, he wants to meet The Four."

They drank in this good news with the Champagne and became euphoric, until Margaret realised the date. "But that's the Saturday of the Art Club Exhibition. You promised to attend. We have been holding back out best stuff for it."

He was pleased to have the power to ease her anxiety. "My dear Margaret," he said. "I have no intention of missing the Art Club Exhibition . . . and neither will Herr Muthesius miss it once he receives your very own pictorial invitation. Oh, and while you're at it you can help me out with my letter of reply."

****

The Macdonald sisters remembered it as one of their happiest and most prolific Christmases and in January the meeting with Herr Muthesius went well. The German, still in his thirties for all he had already achieved, was a charming and attractive companion, a tall, handsome man, impeccably dressed and sporting a full beard and moustache. Margaret thought him a slimmer version of the dashing Prince Edward, who in just seven years' time would become King

Edward VII. Photographs were taken for the Freestyle Architecture book and Muthesius gloried in the Art Club Exhibition and in the whisky and the haggis of the Burns Supper at Margaret's studio apartment. The German talked of a reciprocal visit by The Four, but not to Germany. He wanted to play host to them in Vienna where, he said, the Art Nouveau revolution was gathering pace faster than anywhere else in Europe. It felt as though their ship had come in at last. Not one of them could have foreseen the backlash.

About a week after Hermann Muthesius left Glasgow to return to Berlin, Mackintosh approached his employer John Keppie for certain permissions regarding the Muthesius, book, the granting of which he reckoned would be a mere formality. But they were not forthcoming. On the contrary, Keppie let him know in no uncertain terms that the Herald building and the Queen Margaret Medical College were the firm's work and hinted that Mackintosh's own performance had, of late, been less than satisfactory. He suggested that perhaps the young architect was spending too much time -__ farting about, was how he put it ___ with The Immortals, drinking too much and keeping too many late nights. He referred to the "influence" of the Macdonald sisters. He said that the work they had shown in the Art Club Exhibition had been badly received, that people were calling it depressing and even pornographic. He said their work was "nightmarish" and that the sisters were now notorious. He told Mackintosh that his poster advertising the exhibition of the Glasgow Institute of the Fine Arts was nothing short of disgusting. It showed a cloaked woman grasping a flower which Keppie said was so phallic-looking that it left nothing to the imagination.

It struck Mackintosh that his employer, not a particularly keen patron of the arts by any stretch of the imagination, seemed extremely well- informed. But then it occurred to him that Keppie's sister, Jessie, had a vested interest in destroying the reputation of the Macdonalds and of extricating him from their sphere.

Keppie finished by informing Mackintosh that he had told the same to his friend MacNair. He said it was perhaps time that

Mackintosh decided what he wanted to be ___ a dilettante artist or a serious architect. He told him to take the rest of the day off and that he would see him in the morning.

Mackintosh began to spend more and more time at Margaret's studio apartment. One weekend in early February he began work on a pencil-and-watercolour of his own. Richly symbolic, it showed a large monochrome sun intersected by vague trees. On the right was a narrow cartouche on which Mackintosh practised his new and distinctive printing style. From north to south in two columns it read: THE TREE OF INFLUENCE, THE TREE OF IMPORTANCE, THE SUN OF COWARDICE.

"Why the Sun of Cowardice?" Margaret asked him. "It seems a strange epithet for the benevolent star which gives life to us all."

He stopped work on the piece for the day and turned to smile at her. "My dear Margaret, what could be more cowardly than a yellow dwarf? No, really, I just wanted to convey the constant struggle between good and evil. The sun hides behind clouds. The sun runs every day like a coward from the battlefield and will not wage war with the moon and the stars . . . or with darkness."

"But surely the moon and the stars are his lieutenants," she said. "They help to shed a little light on the darkness in his absence."

Mackintosh found a rag to clean his brushes. "The sun is a coward for entrusting such a task to such small and distant allies. And in the moon, try as he might, he can never revive a dead satellite. In this battle, the moon is already a fatal casualty."

"Your mood seems uncharacteristically pessimistic," she told him. "Is something a amiss?"

He rose from his stool and went to the big window to gaze out at the busy street below. "Perhaps, my dear, I do not know. It's just that, like the sun, I shine, I burn. And yet I am constantly kept under a cloud by forces not meteorological."

"You are still but twenty-seven, Charles," she said. "They won't give you free rein until they consider you have suffered enough apprenticeship."

"Yes, of course," he replied. "But it pains me greatly to have to disappoint Herr Muthesius. I have had to write to him to impress upon him that he cannot, after all, use my name in his new book. I have not yet posted the letter. It is here. I'd be glad if you checked it for spelling and grammar. As you know, they are not my strong points."

He walked over to the coat stand and, extracting the letter from the inside pocket of his jacket, handed it to her. After the usual pleasantries and felicitations she got to the nub of the missive.

It said: *You must understand that, for the time being, I am under a cloud. Although the building in Mitchell Street Lane was designed by me, the official architects are Messrs Honeyman and Keppie , who employ me as an assistant. So, if you reproduce any photographs of the building, you must give the firm's name as the credit, not mine. You will see that this is very unfortunate for me, but I hope that when brighter days come I shall be able to work for myself entirely and claim my work as mine. I think if you were writing to Mr John Keppie, he might give the necessary permissions. I have delivered your kind messages to the misses Macdonald and to Mr MacNair. The pleasure of meeting you in Glasgow was ours and we hope that when you come again we will have the same privilege . . . .*

"The letter is in order," she said, "but I see how frustrating it must be for you. Herr Muthesius was so kind when he was here . . . and so supportive. Frances and I were most encouraged by his positive reaction to the exhibition. I wish we could say the same for the people of this city."

"You mean those patrician dolts who called your work ghoulish," he laughed. "But Herr Muthesius takes a kindlier view, eh? That man can spot a philistine. I fear that he may be our only ally. Heaven knows, I need a friend right now."

She wanted to embrace him, but simply said: "Your portfolio is not healthy?"

"They've given me the Martyrs School," he replied, "but again I've been told to keep it cheap and plain. Of course, I have completed some furniture designs of my own and, if Harvey can make them up in time, I'll be able to show them at the arts and crafts exhibition in April. But I'm struggling to find something that's going

26

to make my name. I'll soon be pushing thirty and they still treat me as a junior assistant. I feel I must leave the firm to progress, but if I do I could be ostracised by the entire profession."

He walked to the window again. On the broad sill stood a vase in which he had concealed a half-bottle of whisky. He uncorked it and took a good swig, then lit up one of his small cigars. She walked over to him and took the bottle from his hand, swigging down a large measure herself. They laughed.

"You are such a tonic to me Margaret," he said. "But there is something that has ben preying on my conscience. I feel that I must also show you this."

From his jacket he removed another letter, this one with a photograph attached. Margaret saw that the picture was of Jessie Keppie.

"I fear that Jessie is having trouble coping with our separation, he said."

She handed the letter straight back to him. "I can't read this," she said. "It wouldn't be right. Just tell me that you have acted honourably by Jessie and have given her no reason for false expectation."

He stubbed out his cigar. "If you are asking if I have used her in any way to advance my position in the firm than the answer is obviously no. Her brother continues to keep me on the tightest of leashes."

She picked up the photograph but appeared to be looking through it. "That will change," she said. "It must, if only by the natural course of events."

CHAPTER FOUR

The School

That evening, the recurring nightmare came. He was a wee boy again, playing hide-and-seek in the Necropolis with his pals and his brothers and sisters. The Necropolis was a great place to play hide-and-seek, and the ones hiding were hardly ever caught. He loved the Necropolis, the main gate of which was just a hundred yards from his home in Fir Park Terrace, his parents' first one together. He had read Poe and many of the other authors of so-called tales of Mystery and Imagination in the penny-dreadfuls and had been deliciously terrified. He had a particular horror of the Premature Burial. He vowed that when he died, he would be cremated. That way, even if he weren't dead but merely in some cataleptic coma, the flames would ensure he would never wake up in his coffin, six feet under the earth. Despite these lurid tales, most of which featured graveyards, he did not fear the Necropolis. At night, he was more in awe of it and, by day, he thought it beautiful. He would take a shortcut through the Necropolis on his way to and from school, marvelling at the sheer variety and ostentation of the tombs. How ornate were these mighty mausolea. How rich these people must have been, made wealthy beyond their wildest dreams by shipping and the tobacco trade. Still, these imposing marble edifices made him and his companions no less irreverent. Some of his more athletic and adventurous pals would even try to climb up the sheer faces of bigger tombstones in an attempt to straddle the top or sit on the wings of some stony angel, undeterred by moss and guano. This was, of course, impossible for him to even attempt, with a few of the less-forgiving boys always making fun of him because his club-foot limp. Gimpy Charlie was what they called him, but that was okay. He regarded most of them as feral idiots and stayed secure inside his own intelligence and the strong sense of integrity bred in him by his policeman father. If only his father had retained some of that integrity for himself.

The dream follows its pattern. At the be beginning of it he is happy and having fun in the game but then, as twilight falls, he finds himself cut off from the others and wonders if they have done the dirty on him again by running off home without telling him. Leaving him in the big graveyard all by himself in the gathering gloom. As he wanders around the Necropolis looking for them, it quickly grows darker, and soon he is seeing only shapes. The myriad mausolea, like child-sized houses, now seem to be SHELTERING the Dead rather than merely covering them. And then what he knows is going to happen unfolds. The stone door of a large vault creaks open and there is light beyond. He cannot stop himself from entering. Inside, he is amazed to find himself looking at one of his own interiors, like the ones he will design for houses he has yet to build. Here is some of his furniture, and there are two gesso panels created by the Macdonalds. In the centre of the room is a large table at which sits alone a ghostly figure. He approaches with trepidation but as he gets closer he sees that it is own mother who sits there and he runs to her in great joy, blinded by tears of happiness and relief. When he asks why she is there, she tells him that

The Immortals have invited her for dinner. He asks if his father has also been invited but his mother seems displeased by this question, telling him that his father can go to hell with his scarlet woman and that she never wants to see the man again. He then asks where are The Immortals? His mother tells him that they very much wanted to come but that it is impossible for them to be there. When he asks why that is, she says it is because they have not yet been born.

He is dumbfounded, frightened, puzzled by her sudden impatience with him. He watches as she picks up the dinner bell and rings it three times. A door at the back of the room opens and in walks Margaret, dressed from head to foot in a white shroud as if for burial. She leads in three men, all dressed as undertakers. The grim faces under the stovepipe hats are grotesque caricatures, yet there is a hint of recognition. Surely the tall one in the middle is Alexander

29

"Greek" Thomson himself, dead these twenty years, the man who designed and built so many of the great edifices of Glasgow. But the other two, he cannot place them, although he has a strong feeling that they also are architects. The grim triumvirate approaches the table and begins to cast exaggerated gestures around the room, ridiculing the furniture, laughing out loud and making insulting remarks about the cretin who designed it. The spectre resembling Thomson points a skeletal finger straight into his face, bellowing "You are the one, You are the one" . . .

The three sit down at the table in a straight line like High Court judges and he finds himself standing in front of them like a prisoner in the dock. He looks for his mother but she has disappeared. He looks for Margaret. He sees her approaching the table bearing a large entrée dish with silver lid. She sets it down in front of Thomson, in whose hands a large carving knife and fork have suddenly appeared. Thomson sharpens them, one against the other. The undertaker architect on Thomson's right lifts the lid of the salver to reveal the severed head of the adult Mackintosh with pennies stuck into the empty sockets where the eyes should be . . .

Mackintosh knew that the Glasgow of his youth was a vast improvement on the slum city of thirty years previously, but he was still only to aware of the spectres of past horrors that every so often would show themselves. Unless you were part of the gentry, you were more than likely to live within, or close to, overcrowded areas of squalor. The immigrants flooded in from Ireland and the Highlands, all looking for work on Clydeside. The ever-expanding urban conurbations could not handle their sheer numbers. Houses were split into rooms which were rented out individually. People existed in tiny and rat-infested living spaces. Some small rooms had as much as three families in them, with no sanitary conditions or running water. Mackintosh never had to suffer anything this extreme but, with eleven brothers and sisters, he would have known all about room-sharing at Fir Park Terrace. Thus was born the vocation to build houses full of space and light. Thus was born the architect. The artist would follow.

His letter to Hermann Muthesius at the beginning of 1895 had been somewhat pessimistic but things improved for him gradually, if not spectacularly, as that year progressed. He enjoyed helping the Macdonalds to find and establish their Hope Street studio and drew closer to Margaret during many summer outings. His relationship with Jessie Keppie trundled on in some kind of a desperate limbo, which troubled him, yet he made no moves to end it despite the fact that it had now become purely platonic. He was drinking more and he blamed it on his dilemma. One bleak Monday morning in January of 1896 he turned up at work with a bad hangover, only to be summoned straight away into John Keppie's office.

He knocked on the door before turning the knob and entering. He was not enthused. His mercifully infrequent visits to Keppie's inner sanctum never failed to depress him. The room was well-appointed but over-stuffed, the chintzy Victorian additions clashing with the predominance of leather upholstery and wood panelling. The high windows allowed plenty of light and were rarely curtained, but on this winter morning the lamps were lit. A cold Glasgow rain battered loudly against the rivulet- covered panes. With the big windows all shut, the over-heated office was stuffy, the general fug unalleviated by the strong pipe-smoke being puffed into the atmosphere by John Keppie, sitting behind his heavy, oak desk studying some papers. Mackintosh knew he was deliberately being ignored, so he lit a small cigar without asking for permission. Despite his headache and the pain in his gammie leg, which played up on damp days, he remained standing because he did not want to sit.

Finally, Keppie turned to him, a big, full-bearded bovine-looking man who, although only six years older than Mackintosh, had the appearance and bearing of being well settled into middle age. His brow was furrowed and the look on his face was one of irritation. Mackintosh had rarely seem the man wear any other expression and resented what he considered to be unnecessary dourness. Keppie came from tobacco money and had been born with a silver spoon in his mouth. The firm was doing well, with James Honeyman practically a silent partner. The employer was formal, austere and soppy-stern, the employee flashy and bohemian. The gulf between the two was plain enough and, of course, there was always the elephant . . . . the elephant by the name of Jessie.

"Ah, there you are, Charles. Take a seat will you, I won't detain you long."

Mackintosh limped soundlessly twards the big desk to occupy the big chair opposite his employer. It was a fierce-looking straight-backed Chesterfield covered in maroon velvet brocade. It had a ridiculous sunken seat. In which the dominutive Mackintosh looked ill at ease. Keppie enjoyed his moment with a look of mild disdain and, as if he didn't know, asked:

"What are you working on at the moment, Chalres? What progress are we making on it?

Mackintosh, already annoyed, felt a swift flush of anger. Why did this pretentious fool think it necessary to toy with him by making out he didn't know what he was working on. He kept his voice level and controlled.

"The Martyrs Public School building, of course John. It is all but completed now. I thought you had the governors' report. I trust that it is favourable."

Keppie leaned forward a little in his big leather chair so that he now towered above his employee across the desk: "Ah, yes, yes, of course, the Martyrs School. You know, Charles, the brats who will be inhabiting this school won't give a toss for all the fine frills you seem to find it so necessary to incorporate. On the contrary, they are more likely to find a barbaric and sadistic glee in pulling them apart. You are aware. I take it, that we are over budget on this."

Mackintosh continued to fight is temper. ""Only by a few per cent, John. The cost of materials fluctuates. We have delivered with time to spare and I have run a daily gauntlet of dealing with the builder McNab and his men. The report is favourable, is it not?"

Keppie said, almost reluctantly: "The report is not unfavourable, Charles. But it annoys me that they seem to think we've given them more than they paid for. A little prudence might help your reputation."

32

Mackintosh decided to stay silent, knowing that any words from him would be bathed in contempt. He wanted to be out of this office, away from the dreadful stuffiness of this man and of his whole philosophy. Suddenly, picking up the papers he had been studying when Mackintosh came to the door, Keppie slung them unceremoniously across the big desk. Instinctively, Mackintosh grabbed them before they scattered on the floor. He knew that had they done so, he would not have given Keppie the satisfaction of stooping to pick them up.

"The new Glasgow School of Art, Charles," said Keppie as if he were talking about an abattoir. "We've been invited to enter the competition for it. A bugger of a commission if ever I saw one. The site is nothing more than a steep slope. The building will have to be shoehorned in like a slanted wedge, but it should be right up your street, as it were." He chortled at his own oh so obvious pun.

Mackintosh peered at his employer from behind the sheaf of papers, afraid now that the look of contempt he had been trying to disguise was as plain as the aqualine nose on his Highlander's face. But then his expression slowly softened and his eyes lit up as he began to arrange the papers carefully, cradling them as if they were his own newborn infant son.

****

He knocked off at five o'clock and, it being a Friday, he headed for a big pub on Ingram Street called the Old Corinthian to meet MacNair. At that time the place was practically empty but later on they knew it would fill up with other office workers and the blue-collar brigade from the Post Office depot. They liked this place because it didn't attract many prostitutes and was spacious, and they enjoyed the half-privacy afforded by the booths. The huge oval bar in the middle of the big cream-and brown painted room was serviced by six apron-clad barmen, so no one ever had to wait long for a drink. Mackintosh felt he had been waiting all his life but that now the wait was over. He smelled and sensed a sea-change.

33

Mackintosh came to their booth with two pints of heavy and went back for the two whisky chasers. "Get that down you," he said to his friend. "We're celebrating."

MacNair smiled, took a big swallow of beer and looked at the papers on the table between them.

"Funny the old man handing you a shot at an art school when he was pissed off about your Martyrs School costings," he said.

Mackintosh thought he detected a faint tone of jealousy. But that was okay. If MacNair were jealous, he would tell him straight out. Their friendship was strong.

"It was Jessie," said Mackintosh. "It had to be. Keppie loathes my artistic ambitions and Jessie wants me to just be a starched architect. But she has her own artistic side. She was in The Immortals after all. I'm sure it was her who convinced her brother that I would make a good job of this, if not a great one. But I am going to make it a great one. You just watch me, Herbie."

He lit one of his small cigars while MacNair puffed on a pipe, both adding to the general fug, despite the comparative sparcity of clientele. As it was still January, the Old Corinthian's six big ceiling fans with massive wooden blades remained switched off.

"Well, there's no doubt it's a bugger of a site, Charles," said MacNair, waving his pipe stem at the papers. "Cheap, steep, sordid and cramped. Mibbe it wisnae Jessie. Mibbe this is some kind of test Keppie's given you. What kind of silk purse are you going to produce from this sow's ear?"

Mackintosh picked up his pint glass and drained it to halfway.

"That's the galling part of it," he said sternly. "If this were just some test of my resourcefulness I wouldn't mind so much if it were just some factory. But this is the city's new art school we're talking about. It should be a jewel, a shining beacon to enlightenment, a testimony to our civilisation . . . perhaps not on such a prime site as the city halls, but certainly not in this hole in the ground up a back street. It just shows you where the city fathers place art on their ladder of priorities."

"Aye well," said MacNair, who revelled in the role of devil's advocate "Oscar Wilde says in preface to The Picture of Dorian Gray that all art is quite useless."

"Aye well," said Mackintosh, tossing off his whisky in a gulp," "Oscar Wilde has obviously never seen the Forth Bridge."

"But why? You won't get any thanks for it, " said MacNair. "Even if you do manage to pull off some minor miracle. You know what those old bastards are like on the board of governors."

Mackintosh felt the first warming effects of the half and half pint. "To shame them, that's why. To show them. To sicken them. They want plainness, I'll give them plainness with complexity. They want cheapness, I'll give them cheapness with extravagance. They want a functional old box, I'll Give them a box of tricks in which nothing will be quite as it seems. Can't you see it Herbie? Don't you realise that this is the i9deal response? Keppie could hardly touch the remit. He slung the papers at me as if old Honeyman had just wiped his arse with them. But by the time I'm finished they'll want to pluck the whole school from its foundations as if by the hand of God and plunk it back down again in the middle of George Square."

"Are you sure that's your first pint Charles?" said MacNair, though he had thoroughly enjoyed the monologue.

Mackintosh decided to give as good as he got. "Drinking with you Herbie, is usually a one-pint experience." He nodded towards his almost empty glass. "I suggest you stand your hand before this evaporates."

CHAPTER FIVE

Blueprints and Whisky

She hadn't seen him in nearly a fortnight. She knew he wasn't going to the Cotswolds this summer. His mother had said so. No, his mother had not seen him nearly a month but he had sent letters saying he was staying at the Empire Hotel. She could not find him at the Empire Hotel and so had decided to walk up to Bath Street, though it was not quite yet eight' o'clock in the morning. It was a pleasant MayDay and, for once, the gutters were running not with rain, but cherry blossom. Nevertheless, she still carried an umbrella and used its handle to bang on the locked front door of Messrs Honeyman and Keppie. After some minutes, she heard the door being unlocked and it creaked open to reveal the head of old Murdoch, the caretaker. He knew her, but gave no sign of recognition. She imagined she'd probably interrupted his morning cup of tea and perusal of the horse-racing newspapers.

"Ah, Mr Murdoch. Do forgive me. I know it's early but I was wondering if Mr Mackintosh was perhaps already at his desk."

Murdoch struggled to fit his ancient pince-nez. "Miss Macdonald, is that you? Mr Mackintosh, you say. Haven't seen him this morning as yet. If anything, he's usually a late arrival."

"Save on those not infrequent occasions when he stays here all night. Mr Murdoch."

This struck the old man as amusing. "All night? No Miss. Wouldn't be allowed. That would never do"

"Do you mind if I go up, Mr Murdoch?, she said. "Perhaps he is simply asleep."

"You can go up Miss, said the old man, "but it won't do you any good. The door will be locked. Mr Keppie has that key and he's not due in until eight-thirty. He . . . . . "

The old man chuntered on but she had already swept past him and was halfway up the stairs on her way to the first-floor assistants' office. Contrary to Murdoch's report, the door was not locked. She entered and moved through the outer chamber to the cubbyhole at the back assigned to Mackintosh. She opened the inner door and saw Mackintosh fast asleep in his chair, his curly head slumped on a desk littered with new drawings. She could smell whisky and then saw the empty bottle in the crammed wire wastepaper bin.

"Tosh, wake up. How long have you been here? I've not seen you in over a week. You're white as a sheet."

He came round slowly and smiled inanely as he looked up at her. "Margaret. I finished late. I saw little point in going back to the hotel. How did you get in?"

"Old Murdoch knows me by now," she said, "but he doesn't know that you are here." She indicated the wastebasket with the whisky bottle. " Go to the washroom while I get rid of this. We've time to get some breakfast at Cameron's. When did you last eat anything, Tosh?"

"Bugger breakfast," he said. "Unless Cameron's will sell us some early-morning Champagne.". He stood up and looked down at the drawings. "It's finished, the first section."

She began to gather the drawings and arrange them into a coherent order and as she did so her expression grew ever appreciative. She grasped that he was designing holistically, so that the inside of the building complemented the outside.

"The new art school, Tosh. It's wonderful, but they'll never be able to afford this."

"Aye they will," he said taking the sheaf of papers from her hand. "The beauty of this design is that I can build the school using only the plainest and simplest of materials. Look here," he began shuffling through the drawings. "No obstructive Greek columns or Gothic arches they can't afford, but huge windows to catch the North light, and plain masonry. The studios behind those windows are twenty-six feet high. And look, Margaret, at the wrought-iron work outside of the windows. Do you not see something of your own there?"

"The long-stemmed roses," she said. "But will they allow it? Won't the governors regard such a feature as a flippant waste of money? "

"They'll allow it when they see that the feature is also functional," he replied. "Not only are the iron roses beautiful, they also serve as holders for the window-cleaners' planks. The difference in cost there will be negligible. Look here," he became more animated. " The layout is a shallow E and there is a central core which holds the services, the admin room and heating chamber as well as the entrance hall and the staircase. Higher up there is the headmaster's room and studio and at the top we pan out into a museum and gallery where the students can display their work. The studios are ranged on either side to catch the North light. Now, look at the two outer wings. Here we have other features such as the library, caretaker's quarters and boardroom. As these wings are falling backwards, as it were, into the slope of Renfrew Street, they will consist of five storeys compared with just the three on the south front. I had to tailor my entire design to the unevenness of the site. Although there will be a difference of two storeys between front and back, you won't see it in the elevation. The slope of the site will hide it."

"I see the wonder of it Tosh, she said. "But the remit was something plain and coarse. You are incapable of delivering such a thing."

"I CAN give them plainness," he said, " but the design itself can hold great magic . Consider the fantastic sculpture contained within the Pyramids of Egypt, or in the construction of a spider's web, or in the perfect nests of small birds or the micro-cities created by certain insects. Their remit is simply survival, but look at the art they make."

"Their art is inadvertent," she said.

"And so is ours," he told her. "Are we not artists because we cannot help it?"

The intensity of their exchange was interrupted by a shuffling in the outer office as Old Murdoch approached.

"You'll be getting me the sack, Mr Mack," said the old man. But it was said with levity. Old Murdoch liked Mackintosh and his woman.

Margaret took it as her cue to leave. "Shouldn't you get some rest, Tosh? Perhaps Mr Keppie could give you the morning off in lieu of finished work."

"Yes," he said. "I fear he must. But don't worry. I'll be fine. I need to consult you about a design for the architrave."

She was immensely pleased by this and only Murdoch's presence prevented her from kissing him. But halfway to the door she turned swiftly on her heel.

"Oh my, I almost forgot," she called to him. "The reason I've been trying so hard to track you down. Kate Cranston came to see Frances and me in our studio yesterday. She wants a word with you."

****

The redoubtable Miss Cranston was not quite what one might expect of a hard-headed businesswoman. A fervent supporter of the Arts and a patron of the Glasgow Style, she looked more an artist's model herself . . . .tall. slim, elegant, fair of face and immaculately dressed. At age thirty-eight she was ten years older than Mackintosh, yet her countenance and egalitarianism lent her a fine youthfulness. She abhorred Victorian chintz and Victorian hypocrisy and adored the avante-garde. The ghostly eroticism of The Four had recently shocked English visitors to the Arts and Crafts Exhibition Society in London, a fact which had delighted Miss Cranston. Already proprietress of several small Glasgow tearooms and coffee shops, she had acquired a large and prestigious set of rooms in Buchanan Street and ghostly eroticism was just what she had in mind for it. Mackintosh had been publishing a lot of his designs for furniture. Miss Cranston admired them greatly, but had already commissioned George Walton. In future projects she would exclusively commission Mackintosh to design everything, right down to the knives, forks and spoons.

She sat regally opposite Mackintosh at a small tea-table in the first-floor gallery of her new establishment as early summer sunshine filtered through the big windows. Some joiners, carpenters and other workmen busied around them.

"Such charming girls the misses Macdonald," she said to him, "and so fearless. And your own work, Mr Mackintosh. I see the Japanese influence there. I heartily approve of your employers' decision to enter your designs for the Glasgow Art School competition and I know you have other important work waiting. But I was hoping you could contribute to this new venture of mine. I've hired Mr Walton for the furniture but I want you to do the lunchroom walls and smoking gallery. From what I've heard, Mr Mackintosh, your watercolour created quite a stir in London, and who can forget this poster you made for the Fine Arts exhibition?"

She unravelled the copy she had brought with her to show the dreaming woman clutching the phallic rose.

Mackintosh felt tired and a little sleepy in the dappled sunlight. He was not entirely sure that he should be designing tearooms and had agreed to meet Miss Cranston because he knew Margaret liked what she was doing and was keen to be involved.

"I trust my poster is not too obvious Miss Cranston. I strive for a certain subtlety."

"Of course," she said. "And there's the wonder of it. Subtlety and discretion at all times, but also plenty of excitement, eh? Oh and by the way, please call me Kate."

He returned her smile was still ill at ease. He began to worry that he might be being hired as some lurid comic-book illustrator. Furthermore, he considered George Walton to be a copycat and plagiarist. On the other hand, he respected her for her support of the Glasgow movement and suspected that she was just trying to be fair by spreading the work around. But his very soul railed against the sub-division of commissions. He was an all-or-nothing man. Margaret was the only exception and he allowed that only because he genuinely felt that they were one.

"George Walton. Miss Cranston . . . er Kate. Is he perhaps not exciting enough for you? Forgive me, but it seems to me that if you are willing to entrust Mr Walton with the principal features of the interior then surely you must also allow him to complete the picture. Is Mr Walton not himself a little disconcerted by the fragmentation of his commission?"

She laughed. "I heard you were a perfectionist Mr Mackintosh, but there are some of us for whom a little sub-contracting is all part of the appeal. Look on ot, if you will, as an introduction. I may have bigger fish for you to fry later on."

He thought of Margaret. They ahd arranged to meet up after this appointment. He knew he couldn't go down to her studio and tell her he had rejected the Cranston woman. She would be so disappointed.

"It may not be the Albert Hall, Mr Mackintosh, or a royal palace," she interrupted his thoughts. "But it will be a fine addition to your native city and enjoyed by thousands of your fellow Glaswegians. We are champions of the Temperance Society, don't you kow, serving, as we do, to keep our citizens away from strong drink. Your Miss Macdonald may also find some scope here, if you do not mind me saying so."

He felt as though she had read his thoughts. "What, in decorating your tearoom, Miss Cranston, or in keeping me sober?"

She laughed again and he was won over. "Whoever enjoyed tea and scones or fulfilled a lovers' tryst in the Albert Hall, eh Miss Cranston? . . . er Kate. I can let you have some drawings by this time next week."

CHAPTER SIX

The Winner

George Walton notwithstanding, the Cranston woman loved Mackintosh's designs for the luncheon gallery and, above it, the smoking chambers, of her big new Buchanan Street tearooms. With the premises on three levels, Mackintosh attempted to give the impression of lower earth, middle earth and sky. The striking feature was the stencilled friezes of four ten-feet tall haloed women enmeshed in rose bushes that lined the gallery's west wall. They flanked an abstract of a tree, which was both phallic and vulva-like. The effect, described in one newspaper as like having tea in Heaven, would certainly give the city dowagers plenty to talk about over their elevenses. While Mackintosh took the credit for it all, the haloed women were, of course, copied from work created by Margaret Macdonald. Mackintosh had insisted she be credited but she had steadfastly refused. She felt his career to be just at the point of taking off and was glad to give any boost. His reputation was growing despite the naysayers. He was now working on the Queens Cross Church for the firm and the announcement of result of the Art School competition was due before the end of the year.

It was Jessie who found it, one day in early December, just lying there on her brother's big desk. Jessie had a part-time job as a secretary at the firm and would always manoeuvre to spend the lunch hour with Mackintosh. The envelope from the Art School Board of Governors lay at the top of a pile of mail. Keppie himself was keeping a luncheon appointment with another client. The envelope had been knifed open at one edge. She extracted the letter and read that the design of Charles Mackintosh had won the new Art School commission for the firm of Honeyman and Keppie, with the provision that Mackintosh himself be installed as principal project architect. She was ecstatic and cradled the letter to her breast like a dowry.

She made up her mind to tell him before the official announcement was made. He was out on a site visit at Queens Cross and she decided to make her way over there. She was a little dismayed when he appeared not to share her ecstasy at the news. It was as if he had been expecting to win and that this was merely official confirmation. He almost seemed blasé about it. She told him that they would have to celebrate. She would book a table at the Grand Central Hotel in Gordon Street, just for the two of them. She knew there would be hell to pay if her brother found out about her sneak preview of the letter, so she cautioned him to tell no one else until the official announcement was made. This also seemed to bore him. But Mackintosh wasn't bored, he was galvanised. This was the moment he had been waiting for. He could not express his joy to her because it wasn't FOR her. But he could now make his intentions clear to Margaret Macdonald. He knocked off at the church early and headed for the sisters' studio.

For once he found her not painting, but struggling with a typewriter. Stenography was not her strong suit.

"I'm glad you're here," she said. Gleeson White, of the Studio magazine, was here. He just needs some more on you to complete his article on The Four. Will you write up a potted biography, Tosh?"

"I fear we must tell Mr White to rename his article," said Mackintosh. "From now on we should be known as The Three, for you and I are one."

For a moment she thought he might have been drinking again. "You know you always work alone, Tosh. You insist on being completely responsible for every aspect of your work. I fear that I may not be up to your standards of excellence. I should hate to disappoint you in any way. . . .if I should do anything to damage our friendship...."

Mackintosh moved around the desk and took her by the shoulders, raising her up until they stood face to face.

"My dear girl," he said. "I had hoped that by now our relationship could by now be called something more than friendship. Don't you

43

know that there is nothing you could do that would disappoint or offend me in any way. My admiration for you fills me up. I revere your work above all others. I feel in my sou that we were meant to work together. You must not consider anything you do for me to be in the way of complementing my work. Rather, you must feel that your work and my own are one and the same, that our combined efforts are part of the same entity. Listen to me, Margaret, these are not the lovesick ramblings of a fly-by-night suitor who will renege when his passion cools. I know with every part of me that there is no other woman on earth who comes close to you and I feel that somehow you were sent to me, that we were always meant to be one, that we are meant to work as one and that everything we make will be the better for us being one. Do you not know what I'm saying, Margaret?. I love you and the art school commission will allow me to marry you."

"You got it, I knew you would," she cried. And then he kissed her and, as she responded, she found his moustache to be no kind of irritant whatsoever. The end of the kiss found her light-headed and stunned, but very happy.

"I have to tell you right away Tosh that I feel the same way about you. But you must retain your separate professional identity. And what about Jessie? She's been waiting so long for to you to make a commitment to her. She expects it."

"I'll tell Jessie first thing tomorrow," he said. "Before she books the celebration dinner."

She released herself gently from his embrace and felt the need to resume her seat. As the full import of his words came through to her, the happiness she had felt was suddenly replaced by a great anxiety.

"You say you are going to marry me, Tosh," she said. "But you will change your mind when I tell you that we could never make a child. There is a madness in my family. Though it has never surfaced in us, Frances and I have sworn that we will never pass it on. I am also terrified that I may not be strong enough to bear a child. The infant mortality rate appals me. I am. I fear, not maternal. My child is my work."

Mackintosh gazed down at her with a look of great compassion. It was true that the prospect of never being a father had come as no small shock to him, but he knew even then that for her he would make that sacrifice.

"Then let your child be my child," was all he said. "And let it be ours souls that procreate."

And then he kissed her again.

CHAPTER SEVEN

Back-Yard Prophet

By the summer of 1898 construction of the new art school had been going on for about eighteen months and was increasingly taking up more and more of his time and energy. He knew almost all of the workmen by name. He liked to judge the temperament of each man to know how it contributed, or did not contribute, to the spirit of his buildings. His victory in the competition paid no immediate dividends. On the contrary, his heavy workload for the firm left him tired and sometimes even bewildered. Certainly, there was no more money. Keppie, if anything, had increased his antipathy towards him since he had broken off his prospective engagement to Jessie. Marriage to Margaret would have to wait a wee while yet. To save money he sustained himself at any of the Cranston tearooms, Kate Cranston having insisted that he would always be her guest. He preferred the one in Buchanan Street. Its ambience soothed his troubled mind and the big tables allowed him to work as he ate. Margaret found him there on a wet Wednesday. As usual, high summer in Scotland was consisting of dark, sticky-hot days of torrential rain. He was so distracted by the papers in front of him that he did not see her approach and she was upon him before he could stand up. He cursed himself for his ill manners, never mind that they were unintentional. She only rested her hands on his shoulders and gently stroked his hair, defying the disapproving frowns of two dowagers nearby.

"What is it, my love?," she said. "You look worried. Is it the school?"

He smiled at her and removed his glasses, fumbling in his waistcoat to find a small cigar. "Aye," he said. "I've just been told there's no money for the west wing. They're going ahead with the main block and the east wing but mothballing the west wing *for the time being*, it says here." He gestured towards the pile of papers on the tea table.

He found the half of a cigar but no matches. "It's a disaster," he said. "My work has to be seen as a whole. The west wing is absolutely integral to the complete design. They're going to leave the west side hanging in mid-air. It will look like a building under demolition, like a man who has lost his right arm and leg . . . . a crippled thing."

She tried to soothe him. "But there will be more money in future annual budgets, Tosh. If you can only wait . . . . "

He took her hand. "No, it's not just the money, my dear. Since the project began I've had a creeping sense of attrition. The only obstacles to this project are the idiots who sanctioned it in the first place. Those penny-pinching old fogies on the board of governors have me on such a tight leash they are choking my original concept. For Christ's sake, the budget is only fourteen thousand as it is. What do they expect me to do with that? Talk about loaves and fishes? You know, Margaret, when I was a wee boy my favourite fairytale was Hansel and Gretel but I soon found out not much later in life that chocolate and marzipan make lousy building materials.

"But Fra Newbery," she said, "The headmaster, He is on the board and he is championing you. It was Newbery who insisted you be installed as principal architect."

"Yes but that was eighteen months ago," he replied. "After the fact, Keppie was always going to be free to undermine me, and that's exactly what he's doing. He has gone over my head with Wilson the foreman on several occasions. They can't seem to forget this business with Jessie. He makes sure that the firm takes the credit for the work I do. I may have been given principal place, but that's only because it's such a damn difficult commission and doled out on a shoestring. And you can bet that if anything goes wrong I'll be saddled with the blame, but if I pull this one off Honeyman and Keppie will take the glory."

She found matches in her bag and lit his cigar for him. He seemed to calm down a bit.

47

"The thing is Margaret, I can't wait. I need a success in my own name . . . . a building success. No one is going to remember me for a newspaper depot and an obscure back-street church. I am thirty years old now and still an assistant. They suck the blood from me. Perhaps we should clear out of Glasgow. How would you like to live in Bavaria?"

He dug to the bottom of the papers on the table and handed her an opened letter. "It's from Muthesius," he said. "The article he wrote on us has been published in Munich. Apparently we have given Glasgow a new face. Well, at least I'm big in Germany."

★★★★★★★★★★★

John James Burnet FRSE FRIBA RSA RA was a man who did not take too kindly to losing. Still only thirty-nine, he had already established himself as the doyen of Glasgow architects by designing and building The Athaneum, Charing Cross Mansions, the Clydeport Building, the Barony Church and the John McIntyre Building for the university. He had badly wanted the new Glasgow School of Art. The Paris-trained Burnet recognised Mackintosh as a prodigious new talent but cared less for Mackintosh the man, despite hardly knowing him. Burnet's Congregationalist-Presbyterian sensibilities were offended by what he'd heard of Mackintosh's womanizing and drinking, and the perceived erotic nature of his designs.

On this hot rainy summer's day Burnet, who retained his seat on the art school board of governors, sat in the smokers' lounge of the Glasgow Gailes golf club at Irvine, scowling at a nervous John Keppie. Both men were dressed in golfing gear but neither fancied going out on course for a soaking. Burnet had invited non-member Keppie ostensibly for a round of golf, but really for a progress report on the school and a check on the activities of Mackintosh.

Burnet took a Havana from his cigar wallet without offering one to Keppie. "For Christ's sake, does the man think we're made of money, John? We commissioned an art school, not a new town hall."

48

Keppie nodded sychophantically. "He treats all buildings the same, JJ --- mediums for his ego. No one wants to see murals of symbolic goddesses on the walls of an ironmonger's warehouse."

Burnet took an envelope from a briefcase and spilled out some photographs. "Some of this furniture of his is ridiculous, never mind impractical."

"Aye," Keppie replied. "You'd need gie short legs to be able to sit on one of those ladder-backed chairs."

"I'm bothered by this kind of frippery in the West Wing," said Burnet. "We can't possibly sanction commencement of work upon it before a review is undertaken."

Keppie looked crestfallen. "But are we not going to cut it , JJ? We must open in six months. We've a commitment to the governors and the city fathers. Mackintosh is such a bloody perfectionist that he already has the firm behind schedule and we're losing money. He has defied me more than once and countermanded instructions I have given to the builders."

"Yet his reputation is growing, eh?" said Burnet, puffing on his massive cigar. "The Herald building, the medical college, the Martyrs School, the Queen's Cross Church and those hellish tearooms he does for Kate Cranston have all been well received. . . and haven't done your firm any harm either, eh John? I also hear that he's established a European link."

Keppie stammered and choked a little on the smoke. "Yes, but . . . ."

"All right, man" interrupted Burnet. "Calm down. In might well be prudent to hold him in check a little. I think it's about time Mr Charles Rennie Mackintosh decided where his true vocation lies. He is either a Scottish architect or a cosmopolitan fancy interiors merchant. I won't let him turn this city into an ersatz Japanese courtyard or a Spanish-American boulevard. Glasgow is Glasgow, right? It's not bloody San Francisco. Oh and by the way, don't worry about the governors. We'll open in six months as planned and without the West Wing"

He cut his cigar and replaced the unsmoked half back into the wallet, then walked to the window to look out the sodden and deserted first tee

"Bloody rain." he said. "No point in your hanging about John. We're not going to get a round today.

As Keppie made his way out of the smoking lounge, Burnet called to him: "You'd better get in touch with the Fire Chief. As far as I can see from the plans, the fire escapes are integral to the complete design and, since we'll be opening with a half-finished building, you might need another certificate."

****

Francis Henry Newbery, headmaster of the Glasgow School Of Art, was a man ahead of his time and, among the students, nothing short of a hero. A   progressive educationalist as well as an accomplished portrait painter in his own right, he would give teaching jobs to real artists rather than certificated professionals, and also employed women in important positions. None of this made him very popular with the governors. Needless to say, he had championed Charles Rennie Mackintosh from the very beginning. By November of the year 1899 Fra Newbery was forty-four years old, a tall and handsome man with thick greying hair and an imposing set of eyebrows and moustache. Margaret Macdonald was happy and relaxed to walk with him around what had so far been constructed of the new school. This November day was blindingly bright, with the winter sun sitting low, allowing strong light to flood into the newly made chambers. As they walked among stacked piles of builders' materials, Newbery and his companion knew that they had entered into the presence of something very special.

Having passed through the entrance hall, they paused for a moment at the foot of the main stairwell. Newbery threw his head back and looked up. "You know Margaret," he said "I feel as though I could levitate to the top floor without any need for stairs or a lift. Light, light, everywhere there is light."

"Yes," she said. "It is a remarkable achievement considering the restraints that were put on him. . . restraints that he is still having to deal with. The mothballing of the second phase hit him hard."

Newbery nodded sadly. "More revisions for Charles to do when he had hoped to turn hs hand to greater things. Yet what could be greater than this. This building plays games with my perceptions. I cannot decide whether I am looking at it or it is looking at me."

His words pleased her and she smiled broadly as their sneak preview continued through the sun-drenched studios, past charming corridors festooned with stained-glass panels and into the light-filled boardroom . . . the first of Mackintosh's "White Rooms".

"You know, Mr Newbery," she said, "none of this would have been possible without your championing of Tosh. Thank you."

"Nonsense, my dear, he said, "I merely supported the best man for the job. I also felt that, given such an unpromising remit on top of a poor site, a touch of genius would be required, and that, my dear, is exactly what Charles has provided."

He noticed that the pleasure she took in these words had actually made her blush and so decided it might be the right time to ask her about something which had become the worst-kept secret in their creative circle.

"I understand, my dear, that Charles and yourself are now something more than collaborating artists. Do I hear the distant peal of wedding bells? Your own situation has become somewhat more solitary without the companionship of your good sister."

It was true that she had been living alone for the past five months since Frances and MacNair had married in June and then moved to Liverpool, where he had accepted the post of art director at the university. Yet she did not feel remotely lonely. Her work at the studio had doubled and she felt closer to Mackintosh than ever before. Still, she blushed at his inquiry.

"Yes, I hope so, she said. "Perhaps the sound of those wedding bells is not so distant. We have picked out a place to live, a charming first-floor flat in Mains Street. We are confident of being awarded the lease."

Newbery sounded surprised. "Lease, my dear? Forgive me if I intrude, but surely rented accommodation in a tenement is no proper home for newlyweds of your status? Charles' reputation is growing. A man of his standing should be able to provide his wife at least a house and a garden and also servants . . . . there must be rooms where he can entertain prospective clients."

She looked down at her shoes, her face suddenly vanishing under the brim of her hat. "No, you see Tosh has never made much money on any of his commissions and he's still a junior partner with the firm. He sends a good proportion of his income to his siter Bella in Tyneside. Her husband died, you know, and Tosh is helping to put her boys , his nephews, through school. So you see Mr Newbery, there really is a more practical side to his fight for recognition. He does love children so . . .. "

This last remark had made her tearful, given her own fear of bearing any offspring. Newbery attempted to cheer her again by expounding once more on Mackintosh's art school achievement.

"Yes I think what Charles has accomplished here shows his great concern for the young. Woul that I were young again, coming here to study. In our country's municipal education of the masses, for which reformists had to fight for decades to achieve, school buildings have become such dismal places. Here, Charles has created a veritable wonderland for the children of dockers and miners who show artistic promise."

As they concluded their short visit the blinding winter sun began to fade into the late afternoon twilight, but still her eyes were shining.

****

December of 1899 made a cold, dreich and rainy entrance as the trams and the citizens alike ploughed their way through streets banked with slush. Two days before the promised grand opening of the city's new art school, Charles Rennie Mackintosh, principal

52

project architect, sat in the hated office of his employer John Keppie studying the opening-day programme and order of speeches. Keppie had drawn up the programme himself and insanely stipulated that everything would be done al fresco. A crude platform would be erected outside the main entrance from which the speakers would have to deliver their monologues regardless of the weather, which was sure to be dismal if not appalling. A big silk ribbon in front of the dual main doors would then be cut. Keppie had been dealt a serious blow by the news that the person who was supposed to be doing the cutting, honorary chair of the board of governors the Duchess of Galloway, had pulled out through illness and that the task would now probably fall to John James Burnet. The absence of the Duchess greatly reduced the prospect of blanket newspaper coverage which would have been, of course, free advertising for the firm of Honeyman and Keppie. But the local press would certainly be there, as would the Glasgow evening papers. There would be speeches from Burnet, Newbery, Keppie and Mackintosh himself. In the afternoon there would be a reception in the main hall, with refreshments and a small orchestra, and in the evening there would be a dance for the students.

Mackintosh hardly gave the programme a second glance. In fact, he somehow felt distanced from the whole affair. Overwork and fatigue, he thought. Christ, he could do with a drink. He was reaching for a small cigar when the door opened and an ebullient Keppie walked in. Keppie was hardly ever ebullient.

"I trust the programme meets with your approval then, Charles. It's just that you seem to have so much else occupying you these days that I wonder if you are still focused on this. It's a bugger about the Duchess not coming."

Mackintosh put his cigar back in its case. "Oh I'm very focused John," he said "especially on the fact that only half of my building is standing. How did you manage to procure a certificate?"

Keppie seemed almost gleeful. "I didn't," he blurted. The Fire Chief and his men will attend and I've had to pay for them to be on guard at the evening dance as well. It will take at least another three weeks to install an interim fire escape system that will allow phase one to be put in use as a working building. As it is, the Fire Department has detailed the number of sand and water buckets we'll need in the main hall."

Mackintosh held his head in hands, trying to control the rage he now felt. He stood up and paced in circles. "What do you mean the Fire Chief will attend. I'll be a bloody laughing stock. When the newspapermen see a line of fire buckets at the grand opening and a lot of firemen standing around with hoses like infantry waiting to charge I'll be laughed out of Glasgow. My God man, can't you see what you've done? It's like the Queen being asked to launch a ship full of holes that sinks as soon as it leaves the slipway."

He leaned forward over Keppie's desk so that they were now face to face. "What confidence is anyone going to have in this building if all they can see at the opening is the massed ranks of the Glasgow Fire Brigade, each man holding a bucket of sand? Well, that's it. I won't have anything more to do with it. I wish to be released of my responsibility as principal architect. You can attribute this one to the firm, John. It shouldn't be too difficult since that's exactly what you've done with all my other work."

Keppie was taken aback, having never before seen his employee react with such emotion. He wondered how to deal with it . . . either sack him or try to placate him. With the grand opening only forty-eight hours away, he decided that the former option was out of the question.

"Look Charles, be reasonable," he said. "It's a simple matter of adding the fire stairs later. There's no question of you being humiliated."

Mackintosh turned and headed for the door. "No you're absolutely right on that point," he said. "I won't be humiliated because I won't be there."

****

A small gathering of around forty people crowded round the foot of the platform on a grey day of dank drizzle. On one side of the platform stood a little girl dressed in her Sunday best and holding a small blue-silk pillow on which rested an ornate golden key. Both had been made for the occasion by Margaret Macdonald and she had told the little girl, six-year-old headmaster's daughter Mary Newbery, that she could keep them after the ceremonies. Little Mary tried to wave to Margaret in the crowd while her father Francis opened the speeches, but failed to catch her eye. For Margaret was preoccupied, anxious and perturbed, constantly craning over her shoulder to the street beyond. Mackintosh was a no-show.

From the platform, Newbery saw her agitation and, cutting short his speech, went down to her. "I can't say he's ever been this late before," he said.

"I've not seen him in two days," she replied. "Although I know he was at work on Thursday. It's just as well the Duchess called off. Think of the embarrassment."

On the podium, John Keppie had reached the part of his speech in which he was thanking the Fire Department. He hadn't told anyone about Mackintosh's petulant declaration of two days previously and had simply assumed the man would never carry through his threat not to turn up, knowing what the consequences could be for him. Margaret watched as Keppie chuntered on about safety measures, and then suddenly she knew that Mackintosh would not be coming. Newbery was startled to see her staring at Keppie, her expression hardening into something that could have been hatred.

She attended the dance that night. She now felt that somehow she would have to represent him. There were punchbowls and some of the students had smuggled in whisky. It being a Saturday night, the mood was merry and the orchestra had become more of a fiddle band, with racy jigs the order of the party. A group of half-drunk male students were discussing Margaret, her white dress contrasting impressively with her red hair. One of them dared another to ask her for a dance. Emboldened by the drink, the young man approached her. He was taller than Mackinosh, almost as tall as she was herself. She accepted his hand without word or expression, like an automaton, and they took the floor. As the fiddle music reached a crescendo, the young man became somewhat over-enthusiastic and tried to whirl her off her feet. She spun with him, faster and faster, her face a picture of abject misery.

CHAPTER EIGHT

Ms Cranston To The Rescue

Mackintosh was also dancing, but not with art students. He sorely missed his friend MacNair and, paralytic at the nadir of a two-day drinking binge, found himself in the bar of a dockside whorehouse and pulled on to the spit-and-sawdust floor by the Great Unwashed. One of them tugged at his clothes, trying to grab his pocket watch, and he lashed out. Others laughed uproariously at his club-foot limp. He had caught the would-be watch-thief with a hefty back-hander that had knocked the scoundrel over and he knew that consequences would be inevitable. As three toughs approached him from the other side of the saloon, a young woman grabbed his hand and led him up a flight of stairs to a damp and dingy bedroom, saving him, for the time being at least, from a certain beating. The place had an unwritten code that whoring always took priority over fighting.

Even through his drunken haze he could make out that she was less ravaged-looking than most of the others and thought that she must be very young, probably still a child.

"That mob is no company for a professional gentleman like yourself," she said. "You've been telling everyone you are an architect. Houses is it?"

"Houses, yes. Houses of ill-repute apparently," he gave a weak laugh. "Whisky, I must have some whisky. Give me the bottle . . . ."

The girl wanted to tell him he'd already had enough. She had taken a bottle from the saloon downstairs and now he roughly pulled it from her grasp. He uncorked it and took a big slug. It hit him like a wrecking ball and he collapsed on to the ramshackle single bed. She slapped his face a few times but he appeared to be comatose.

"Architect is it?" she said under her breath. "Well, you certainly had plans for that poteen."

She went through his pockets but found only two florins, amounting to four shillings in money, and his address book and pen. She wanted to take his pocket-watch but somehow could not bring herself to do it. She thought him handsome and she felt sorry for him. She couldn't understand how a man with a limp would also want to stagger. She took one of the florins and the half-full bottle of whisky and went back downstairs to the saloon.

He was not unconscious for long and came to some twenty minutes later disturbed by someone trying to turn him over. He opened his eyes to find himself being fleeced by the watch-thief. The creature apparently had a good eye. The timepiece was Vacheron Brothers, Swiss 18-carat gold passed down to him by his father when he turned twenty-one.

He lashed out again with his right elbow, catching the man on the side of the head, and the robber backed off, howling. But now there were three others in the room, the hardmen he had seen downstairs.

Those who pitied him for his limp could not have known that it was no real handicap. He had never sobered up so quickly, and now he ran for the door, slamming it shut behind him as he bolted down the stairs. It was lucky for him that the hardmen in pursuit were well-sodden with drink themselves and no one in the saloon tried to block his way as he made for the swing doors that would take him out on to the cobblestoned street. The young prostitute, somewhat the worse for wear herself now on the strength of his two shillings, cackled after him that she had been pleased to make his acquaintance and that she hoped he would come again soon. Two shillings could buy her a lot of gin. Once outside, he paused to catch his breath, but two of the hardmen had gained the street via the building's decrepit old fire escape and were now almost upon him. He broke once more into his strange, loping run but he knew he wouldn't be able to keep it up for long. He had just about made up his mind to find a half-brick and turn to face his pursuers when a brougham drawn by a black horse whipped on by a top-hatted driver hurtled across from the other side of the street and drew up beside him. The pavement-side door opened and a vaguely familiar voice urged him to "get in, quick" and soon they were riding off into the misty blackness of the Broomielaw. He slumped down into comfortable leather, happy to rest his aching leg, and turned to see the face of Kate Cranston, inches from his own and smiling broadly.

"My dear Mr Mackintosh," she teased, "is this how you spend every weekend?"

His emotion went from relief to embarrassment. "Miss Cranston, but how . . . .?"

She interrupted him. "As you can imagine, Mr Mackintosh, my tearooms are very popular with the Temperance Society, some of whose braver and more zealous opponents of the demon drink preach the word down in these parts with their sandwich boards and bibles. You were spotted going into that den of iniquity and I was told about it. It could only have ended one way and it appears I was just in the nick of time. And, by the way, your absence from the art school opening ceremony has worried many people, chiefly, of course, Miss Macdonald. What made you do it?"

He turned away from her and gazed out of the carriage window, although there was nothing to see in the gaslight gloom. "It was the fire buckets," he said. "I could have stood for anything apart from that. What kind of reputation is a man to have if he is admitting to the world that his buildings are all but ready to catch fire? It was a joke."

"Do you blame John Keppie?" she asked him.

"Well, he had total control of the actual construction process and schedule," he said "Subject, of course, to my finely detailed plans."

She moved across so that she now sat opposite him, forcing him to look at her. "You've not had much of an easy time of it when it comes to the Keppies and buildings, have you Charles? He seems to be using your genius to take credit for his firm and is niggardly about backing you up when it comes to the crunch."

"Margaret has genius," he said. "I have only talent."

"Still," she pressed on, "you don't need this aggravation. Why not just concentrate on interiors? You and Miss Macdonald could go into business for yourselves. I can introduce you to a lot of potential customers."

He looked away again. "No, I'm going to make my name as an architect, as one of the greatest architects, and there's an opportunity coming up which could establish me nationally if not globally. The new Anglican Cathedral at Liverpool. I'm going to make it mine. I'm going to beat the English at their own game. It will be the making of me."

She took him home to Mains Street, graciously deflecting his many declarations of profuse thanks. She told him it was just between him and her. As he alighted from the carriage, he gave a small groan of pain . . . but then a wail of exasperation.

"My watch . . . my father's watch. It's gone. Those scoundrels . . . ."

"An expensive evening then," she admonished. "Such evenings you cannot afford. especially if you seek reputation."

She made a mental note to buy him a new pocket watch for his thirty-third birthday.

****

Fra Newbery was looking at his watch and shivering in his greatcoat. It was one of those bone-dissolving March days that seem peculiar only to Scotland, with a whipping wind blasting straight off the North Atlantic, up through the Firth of Clyde and straight into his face. Fitting then then he should find himself in a place called Windyhill. He longed to be back indoors in front of a warming fire and hoped this particular little ceremony would be over quickly. With him on this exposed promontory overlooking the small town of Kilmacolm were his host and hostess William and Jean Davidson, and Charles Rennie Mackintosh who, recommended by Newbery, was building the Davidsons a house. Margaret Macdonald made up the group of five and no March wind could have chilled her. She seemed to glow in the light of the engagement ring that now sparkled on her ungloved finger. Mackintosh had bought it on the strength of this commission.

Jean Davidson, a woman in her early forties, was breaking the sod with a spade that seemed way too big for her to handle, while the others mooched around drinking tea and whisky from flasks. Finally the spade became stuck in the hard earth, like Excalibur in The Stone, and Jean was no King Arthur.

"All right, leave it like that," said her husband. "It looks kind of symbolic".

If symbolic was an over-used term in the company of any of The Four, Davidson did not seem aware of it. He was a strict Presbyterian businessman, a Glasgow provisions merchant who had made his fortune on thrift.

But he was by no means a soulless man. He hated the clutter and claustrophobia of Victoriana and admired Art Nouveau and the Glasgow School . His support of it had led to his developing a friendship with Newbery. Now in his late forties, it was time for him to build a house . . but not just any old house. This would be the house for raising his children and looking after his wife and the house that he would retire in and die in. At least that's how he saw it at the time. And because this house would be no ordinary abode, it would need an extraordinary architect. Did Fra Newbery know of such a person? While the Davidsons loved the transformation of the Cranston tearooms, they looked on it as what it was . . . interior design. Windyhill, on the other hand, was the whole deal . . . . the building, the interiors, the gardens, everything right down to the furniture and the kitchen cutlery. Even more reason, Newbery had told him, to give the job to Mackintosh.

Jean Davidson went to the boot of the Rambler automobile her husband had had imported from America and returned with Champagne and five flutes on a silver tray. Mackintosh put away his hip flask and drained his wine glass in a gulp. He stumbled like a drunkard as his bad leg crossed a pothole. Weak jokes were made about the potency of the wine but Davidson felt that his architect was looking the worse for wear.

"Are you all right, Mr Mackintosh," he said. "Perhaps we should return to Glasgow straight away to give you the chance of some rest."

Mackintosh, who was really quite sober, demurred. "No, no I feel just fine," he said. "Not been getting much sleep that's all. Revisions for the art school and the Daily Record building."

Jean Davidson interjected. "Would you like some more time before you start on the house, Mr Mackintosh. If your schedule is such that . . ."

"No, no dear lady, not a bit of it," he said. "This project is just what I need to relax me. It will be a sheer joy, I assure you, to create Windyhill . . . a welcome diversion from the public utility, house for an art lover and a home for a vibrant family. Margaret and myself are both very excited about it. I am ready to submit the plans for the Daily Record warehouse tomorrow and, after that dear lady, I am entirely at your disposal."

Margaret said: "Perhaps we could offer these good people tea back at Mains Street, that is if there is no great rush for them to return to their Glasgow house."

Mackintosh knew she was excited about what they done at Mains Street and that she wanted other people to see it.

"I think you just want another ride in that horseless carriage," he said.

They packed up and drove down to the railway station, leaving the spade protruding from the ground like a claim stake, and when Jean Davidson saw what they had done to their tenement flat at 120 mains Street she couldn't stop smiling for a fortnight.

CHAPTER NINE

Vienna 1

They were married at Episcopal Church in Dumbarton on a hot grey day in late August with only a select few in attendance outside of their immediate families. The MacNairs, of course, had arrived from Liverpool and were being put up by Fra Newbery, but John Keppie was perhaps not such a conspicuous figure by his absence. His sister Jessie, who for these last seven years had harboured hopes of a full and loving reconciliation with Mackintosh, was inconsolable and Keppie had fears for her mental health. Mackintosh himself would brook no conscience. His treatment by the firm was more ambivalent than it should have been and the whole thing with Jessie smacked of an arranged marriage . . . . anathema to him and something which should perhaps be confined to certain Indian religions.

Indeed, he had stopped brooding altogether and had stopped getting drunk. It had been a good summer and work on the art school was going well. He had married the only woman he knew he ever would marry and now he had another announcement to make to the wedding party gathered at a nearby small hotel. The Four were going to Vienna.

Be it serendipity, or even synchronicity, he felt that the Eighth Vienna Secession Exhibition occurring so soon after their marriage and their creation of the wondrous interiors at 120 Mains Street was yet further evidence that he had emerged from his slump. Josef Hoffmann's letter had arrived like a wedding present. Notwithstanding their short four-day honeymoon on the Isle of Arran, would they please honour the Kunstgewerbeschule by addressing its students. They were also invited to take part in the exhibition itself. Mackintosh would exhibit a furnished room. They would be staying with the rising-star secessionist architect Hoffmann during their three weeks in Austria. They all knew it was too good an opportunity to pass up. MacNair had no trouble getting the time off from the university and Keppie would actually be glad to see the back of Mackintosh for a week. Besides, he knew this sort of thing could benefit the reputation of his firm, whether or not it ever worked in Europe.

They left Glasgow on October 11 and In London they took the boat-train to Dover. There followed a rough Channel crossing that MacNair spent lying in a cabin bunk. They spent the night in Paris, where there had been a telegram from Hermann Muthesius. He was very sorry but his multitude of commitments for the exhibition meant he would be unable to meet them. Could they please make their own way to Hoffmann's house.

Their train chuffed into Centralbahnhof on a benign late afternoon on October 14. It was cold, but very still and there was a light dusting of snow on the Ringstrasse. It was the kind of twilight that enhanced Vienna's already considerable charm and the two women were immediately rapt, enchanted by the woinderful sense of space that was so unlike Glasgow and Liverpool. Everywhere, it seemed, there were ornate horse-drawn carriages on the wide boulevards and bandstands of musicians on streets that seemed interspersed with parkland. Dancers and ice-skaters abounded and there seemed a never-ending proliferation of cake-shops. The two men were as yet unmesmerised and more bothered about finding some kind of transport. They had managed to find a porter who wheeled their luggage as far as the station's main exit , but their German was poor and they were having trouble hailing a cab.

The travel-weariness began to take hold. Mackintosh sat down on his trunk and fished in his pockets for a small cigar, but before he could light it two landau carriages bedecked in flowers came hurtling from across the street and descended upon them. The saw right away that one was driven by a grinning Muthesius and the other by a dark, handsome young man whom they would soon discover was their host

Josef Hoffmann. Running behind the carriages came a throng of young people, gaily-dressed and in party mood, swigging from bottles of wine and chanting Mackintosh's name as if he were some great Teutonic hero.

Well, he was certainly a hero in Vienna. . . at least to these young art students, many of them sworn disciples of Hoffmann and other figureheads of the new movement. A flabbergasted Mackintosh and MacNair were then lifted on shoulders before being deposited in Hoffmann's carriage beside their wives, while other students loaded their luggage into the carriage driven by Muthesius.

Hoffmann whipped up his two horses and turned to smile at them. Like most well-to-do Viennese, he had been taught how to speak English from kindergarten.

"Frau Mackintosh, Frau MacNair, Herr Mackintosh, Herr MacNair. Welcome to Vienna. I will now take you to my house where I have arranged a modest reception in your honour."

They moved through beautiful wide streets with some of the students spreading petals in the path of the horses, so that progress was slow. Some of the citizens of Vienna gathered in small groups to ask themselves who could be the VIPs. Hoffmann turned again to catch Mackintosh drinking-in the buildings.

"Impressive but outmoded, eh, Herr Mackintosh? Like those of Greek Thomson who built Glasgow. An anathema to you. But this city is spreading out. They are building on le left bank of the Danube now. A great chance for us "

As if to mimic Hoffmann's mention of the great river that crossed two continents, a bandstand orchestra began playing The Blue Danube by Johann Strauss. This especially appeared to delight Frances.

Hoffmann sneered. "A beautiful piece Frau MacNair, but Herr Strauss was being sarcastic. The stinking old Danube has not been blue for generations."

Hoffmann's villa in Stephanstrasse was not ostentatiously large but seemed very spacious because the interiors were all his own. The Japanese influence was everywhere and The Four could see a lot of themselves in the many stripes and florals. Hoffmann's indulgences were his large drawing room and library. These served as a centrepiece, with six bedrooms surrounding them. His landscaped garden was another source of pride.

In the beauty of their rooms, The Four's travel-weariness lost its exhausting edge. It was, in any case, a fait-accomplis. A reception had been laid on for them and, besides, they were in need of food and drink. Dress would be formal.

Hoffmann's drawing room was more like a ballroom. A small orchestra played Strauss, a magician and an acrobat performed and two long tables groaned with food and wine. The bright young things of the Secessionist art movement danced waltzes under the shimmering splendour of gas-lamp chandeliers. The Four descended from their rooms on a curving staircase. Awaiting them at the bottom of it were Hoffmann and Muthesius. Suddenly, the orchestra stopped playing, the dancers stopped waltzing and a guard of honour was formed. Hoffmann offered his arm to Margaret and Muthesius did likewise to Frances. Mackintosh and MacNair brought up the rear.

As they walked into the dazzling room the young people in the guard of honour began to applaud. None of The Four could quite believe it. They had no idea that they were in this country so revered. Just then it all became a bit too much for Frances, who had been holding on to Hoffmann rather too tightly. Now she forcefully broke away from him and swooned into a dead faint. But before she hit the red carpet a blond man dashed out of the guard of honour and caught her up in his arms.

MacNair and Margaret were quickly by her side, while Muthesius called for some reviving cherry brandy. Frances came round almost as quickly as he had passed out and, seeing that she was going to be all right, Mackintosh and Hoffmann kept their distance. The orchestra started up again and the dancing resumed.

"The younger Miss Macdonald, or should I say Frau MacNair, seems to have an admirer already," Hoffmann said to Mackintosh. "Herbert has competition, no?"

"Who is that blond man who caught her," asked Mackintosh. "He looks most distinguished."

"Ah, you mean his scar," said Hoffmann. "He got it fighting a duel. He killed his opponent. Yes, he is certainly distinguished, if only by infamy. That blond man, my dear Mackintosh, is none other than Max Wolf, adviser and right-hand man to our mayor Karl Lueger, who happens to be one of the most anti-semitic politicians in Europe."

"You mean he is against the Jews?" Mackintosh felt embarrassed by his own rhetorical question.

"More than that, he hates us," said Hoffmann, deadpan.

"My dear Hoffmann, I had no idea . . . " began Mackintosh, but, sensing his guest's uneasiness, the gracious host quickly interrupted.

"It's all right, Charles," he said. "Yes, I am a Jew and there are other Jews here. . . even some very prominent ones. Over there, for example, with the hairpiece. That is Theodore Hertzl, the founder of Zionism no less. And over there in the corner, that bearded fellow is Sigmund Freud. Perhaps you have heard of him in Glasgow, no? Certainly he is making waves in London with his theory of psychoanalysis."

Mackintosh had not, up until that point of his life at least, given much thought to the persecution of European Jews, But he certainly knew what it was like to be denied certain freedoms.

"Why invite this Wolf?" he asked. "Mayor or no mayor?. Why consort with men who have such inhumane agendas, who are, in fact, your enemies?"

"Art cuts across many boundaries, my friend," said Hoffmann. "Mayor Lueger is a zealous Catholic reactionary who hates liberals as much as he hates we Jews. He won't even allow pan-Germans into his administration. Yet Wolf is a German. Perhaps that should tell you something. Anyway, we need the mayor's support for the Secession. There are plenty of factions in Vienna who would close us down completely. Metternich's nephew would send in the army. Some surrealist painters have been branded pornographers. But the contradiction of Lueger is that he is a modernist. He is trying to drag the Austro-Hungarian empire out of its nineteenth-century malaise and devolve more power to the Balkans. He is terrified of the communists and of the foothold Marxism is gaining in some of our smaller protectorates. But his support of new art makes him popular despite his Catholic conservatism."

He paused to lift two Champagne flutes from a passing liveried waiter.
"Perhaps you can empathise with us, Charles. The Jews have always been outcasts but still we have risen against all the odds. In your own country, you yourself are an artistic outcast but still you have transcended the insults."

Hoffmann put his free arm around the Scotsman. "I think this makes us both heroes, no?"

They both burst out laughing and then drank their wine. They joined the others and he immediately asked Frances if she was feeling better.

She nodded, smiling, and said: "Charles, I wanted to introduce you to Herr Wolf but he seems to have disappeared. Oh, how kind everyone is. We may never go home."

They talked of the exhibition, which was to open in two weeks at Josef Olbrich's "Golden Cabbage" purpose-built Secessionist building, and they talked of furniture. It would be the first time the Secessionist Exhibition would feature furniture. Hoffmann introduced Mackintosh to a tall dark man who had a particular interest in the subject. It was in fact the man who had made their journey to Vienna possible.

"This is Fritz Waerndorfer, Herr Mackintosh. He is a successful businessman and patron of the Viennese arts. He was in Glasgow in January and his telegram convinced me that you should be here and convinced the committee to cover your expenses."

"I wish to thank- you sir, and also on behalf of my friends," said Mackintosh. "We are so happy to be here and would not have missed it for the world."

Waerndorfer flushed. Despite his money, he was clearly a modest man, yet still only thirty-three, the same age as Mackintosh.

"Herr Mackintosh," he said. "I am a great admirer. Forgive me, but I cannot put of what I must say to you. I know that this is neither the time nor place to discuss business but. . . . "

Hoffmann interrupted. "He wants you to design and build him a music salon, Charles, for his new house on the left bank. I offered to do it for him but he's been waiting to ask you for most of this year."

Mackintosh had to admit that the idea appealed.

"My first concern, Herr Waerndorfer, would be compatibility. I would of course prefer to design and build the entire house. What will a Mackintosh room look like in a house made by Hoffmann?"

"I should think it would complement it admirably," said Waerndorfer. "It is because of compatibility that I have sought you out. Perhaps we could arrange a day for you to view the plans, the drawings for the interiors . . . "

Mackintosh let the Austrian prattle on with one eye cocked for Margaret, knowing that she would be keen to be involved in the design of a music room. He saw that she had moved some distance away and was being introduced by Muthesius to the small bearded man in the corner their host had named as Sigmund Freud. The great neurologist was at this time forty-four years of age but already bald and with a grey beard and moustache. Margaret thought he looked no less distinguished.

"I am thrilled to meet you Herr Freud, she said. "It is only last month I was reading about your work in one of the London magazines. It left a strong impression upon me."

"Probably sensationalist claptrap," he said. "I'm afraid that I am powerless to prevent my publishers in London from passing on lurid rubbish to the pulp papers. They are trying to raise my profile but, believe me Frau Mackintosh, I have been exposed enough. The effect is that I will come to be regarded as some publicity-seeking charlatan and that my theories will be laughed at."

She sought to reassure him. "Oh no, good sir, the article I read gave a serious treatment to your work and profile. The magazine took a responsible and professional approach journals."

"Thank-you," he smiled, "But still my theories tend to furnish idle dinner-table chatter rather than inspire new treatments."

"Like hypnotism, for instance?"

70

Freud reddened, certain he was being ridiculed. . "If you will excuse me, Frau Mackintosh, I think I will say my farewells. I often work in the evenings. I am only here because Klimt's work interests me. He says that with his nudes he paints the Naked Truth, but I suspect he is harbouring some kind of Oedipus Complex."

She was mortified. "Oh please forgive me, Herr Freud. I am often chided for being too direct, though I mean everything I say. Please stay. There is something I wanted to ask you . . with your permission, of course."

He was somewhat mollified by her obvious embarrassment, and emotion he knew could not be faked.

"Yes, I thought there might be," he said. "I am seldom tracked down by tall, elegant, intelligent women. You can ask."

She had no time, or need, of preliminaries. "I wanted to ask you, Herr Freud, if you believe insanity to be hereditary?"

He did not beat about the bush. "Yes," he said. " I believe certain traits of eccentricity can be passed on in the genes. But this is not really my field. It is by no means certain, or even likely, that a madman or woman will have mad offspring. There is a school of thought that questions if there even is such a thing as insanity, the argument being that it is only relative to sanity and who's to say what is sane?"

The short silence between them was not uncomfortable, Eventually, Freud said: "You are newly-married, yes?" She nodded. "And you are wondering whether or not to have children because there is insanity in your family, is this not so?"

Despite his reasonable inference, she was still taken aback. "You have been talking to my husband?"

"No, no, dear lady, I have not yet had that pleasure. Please do not look so shocked. To correctly arrive at what is troubling you was a simple deduction."

"So you are a detective as well as a psychiatrist," she smiled.

"I prefer the term neurologist," he said. "I suppose that I am something of a rarity. . . . the world's only consulting head-shrinker. You see, it sounds like something from a circus nomatter how I dress it up. But then, psychoanalysis is in its infancy, People are terrified of what they do not understand."

"May I ask who it is that consults you, Herr Freud. What kind of patients, if I may call them so."

"Patients, yes, to the extent that I do occasionally administer medication, but clients is what they would prefer to be called. All have one thing in common, Frau Mackintosh, that, whether they realise it or not, they are all inwardly in turmoil, railing with all their souls against something they may not even be able to identify. It is my job to break down the resistance, to reveal the hidden conflict. Only then can we start with treatment. They come from all walks of life, from chimney sweeps to duchesses to. . . . . artists. But it is a Pandora's Box. I often think there are some neuroses better left buried. Sometimes the operation will kill the patient, eh? Still I have not yet lost anyone. Tell me, Frau Mackintosh, what is it that you are railing against?"

She wondered then if he were flirting. "You are the master of deduction, Herr Freud. Why don't you tell me what my conflict is."

"Probably something originating in childhood, as in the majority of cases. For example, did either of your parents sexually abuse you? Did you witness your father trying to kill your mother, or vice-versa? Is this what you are blocking out?"

She swooned a little, heady now with the wine she had drunk. But before she could reply to him, they were interrupted by a bearded young man with intensely staring eyes, whose hair seemed to falling out in clumps. He was poorly dressed and had evidently not long finished working. There were still streaks of paint on his face and forehead. Despite this, Freud seemed pleased to see the man and attempted an introduction, but the man spoke first.

"You are the May Queen come to life," he said to her. "I knew it must be you. I have seen the triptych you created for the Glasgow tearoom and now that I see you in the flesh I see that it also a self-portrait."

Freud nevertheless took it as his duty to persist in the formalities. "Frau Mackintosh, may I present Gustav Klimt, revered artist of this land and leader of the Secession movement we have all gathered here to celebrate."

She offered her hand and he kissed it, but his piercing cobalt eyes never left hers. She was sure she must be blushing now, in the throes of a hot flush. This small triumvirate was clearly one of mutual admiration.

"You are a great man, Herr Klimt," was all she could muster. "You have put your country on the map of progressive art In Europe and opened doors for many of your young contemporaries. It is an honour to make your acquaintance."

"The honour is all mine," he retorted quickly. "I hope you will not think it rude of me to dispense with your married name for now and call you by your own one, for it is in your work that I have found some of my greatest inspiration."

"Careful of that Oedipus complex, Gus," said Freud. "This woman is not your mother and you will have to come to terms with the fact that she has married another man and taken his name."

"And only three months ago," said Klimt. "I know much about this woman. I read all of Muthesius's articles in Ver Sacre."

73

He released her hand. "Ziggy thinks I wanted to fuck my mother but he is wide of the mark. No one would have wanted to fuck my mother. Not even my father. But talking of Oedipus, I discern a certain Greek influence in the paintings of Ms Macdonald, eh Ziggy, which must be anathema to her new husband who railed so loudly against the buildings of Alexander Thomson, the man who tried to turn Glasgow into Athens."

Somehow, she did not in the least mind him talking about her as if she were not there.

"Yes, it's true, I have never kept notebooks," she said. "My inspiration is all in my imagination and this comes from reading Homer's Odyssey and also the Celtic Legends and other folklore."

"Denizens inhabited by goddesses, satyrs, sirens and nymphs, are they not," said Klimt. "I knew we were the same. And yet we have suffered from the same ignorance and philistinism. . . just like my friend Ziggy here."

Freud seemed to have forgotten about his previous pressing engagement. "He is talking about the public reaction to the three paintings he delivered for the ceiling of the great hall of the university. . . .Philosophy, Medicine and Jurisprudence. All featured nudes engaged in certain poses and gestures which the establishment found disturbing and unwholesome. I thought they were wonderful. But there was condemnation right across the board.... political, aesthetic and religious. . . . and in the end the university refused to hang them. Somehow, he still has the support of Mayor Lueger but is refusing to accept any more public commissions. Is this not so, Gus?"

"Ms Macdonald has suffered a similar reaction to her work," he said. "The only nudity I paint is the Truth. The Naked Truth, to rebel against an Austrian society that buries its head in the sand like an ostrich and ignores all social and political problems."

74

She burst out laughing, wondering if that was why the country was called Osterreich.

But just then the smiles were wiped off all of their faces when they were approached at speed by a frantic Herbert McNair, clearly in a state of some agitation. Mackintosh, Muthesius and Hoffmann were not far behind.

"Oh Margaret," wailed MacNair. "Listen to me. Have you seen Frances? I've searched the whole house. Did she tell you she was going out? We can't find her anywhere."

CHAPTER TEN

Vienna 2

"For God's sake Herbert, how could you have lost her?. She's not a cigarette case. Surely she can't be far."

MacNair visibly wilted under this scolding from his sister-in-law.

"I assure you she is not in the house, Frau Mackintosh," said Hoffmann. "I fear we must now look outside for her."

Freud interjected. "Forgive me, but may I offer a suggestion. The young Frau MacNair has tonight made a friend of Max Wolf, has she not? It may be significant if he is also no longer here."

"You're surely not suggesting that they have run off together, man," said Mackintosh. "She is not long married and has a six-month-old baby being cared for by her family in Glasgow."

"My apologies," said Freud. "I am delighted to meet you Herr Mackintosh. I mean to cast no aspersions on Frau MacNair. It's just that this man Wolf is a very persuasive fellow, and most aptly named. He can be reckless and is not without a certain vicious charm. I wouldn't put it past him to take the young lady away without anyone's permission, such is his arrogance. Perhaps you should try his house. It is one of the biggest and most ostentatious on the Karlsplatz."

They interviewed the servants. It was ascertained from a footman that the old janitor had seen a young couple touring the wine cellar and that they had then left by the cellar door, Yes, the janitor was sure that the blond man was Max Wolf.

"Muthesius can take you to his house, Charles," said Hoffmann. "The likes of Dr Freud and myself would not be welcome there. Please forgive me, my friend. I had no idea that even Wolf would stoop so low as to attempt something like this. But then, he could be trying to provoke me. His anti-semitism is well known. Since you are guests in my house, something like this could make me look bad. Public image is Wolf's speciality, That's why Mayor Lueger employs him. Also his unbridled lust may have been set aflame by the Macdonald sisters' association with art that has been labelled pornographic."

It was only a five-minute walk. Mackintosh limped but he was still some yards out in front of the other two. MacNair had seemed a bit drunk and the cold, fresh air hit him hard. His wife was missing, but he was bringing up the rear.

At the gate, the two Scots were halted by armed policemen but Muthesius was allowed to pass and made his way up the long, curving drive. At the door he was halted by the butler, but the lithe and powerful Muthesius easily pushed his way into the hall. When he stormed into Wolf's library, it appeared that he was just in time. Frances was reclining on a chaise longue with Wolf leaning over her.

She looked somewhat dishevelled and he had removed his jacket, tie and waistcoat. On the table beside them sat two empty Champagne glasses, but Muthesius was horrified to see something much more sinister .... an opened syringe case and a small vial containing what he suspected to be a solution of cocaine. He felt outraged, but knew it was important to stay in control. He felt a calm disposition was his best hope of resolving this situation without further calamity.

He continued to speak in English. He felt it was important for Frances to be able to follow what was going on so that it might bring her to her senses.

"Excuse me, Herr Wolf," he said, "but the lady's husband is at your gate. May I suggest a tactical retreat."

He cast a worried sideways glance at the drugs apparatus on the table and was relieved to note that the solution had, apparently, not yet been administered.

Wolf was furious at being disturbed. He turned around slowly, slurring his words and looking the worse for wear.

"Oh it's you, Muthesius, the sanctimonious little diplomat. How the hell did you get in here? No, don't bother telling me, just get the hell out."

Frances began to giggle at this, but then rolled over and fell off the couch before vomiting on the carpet, her ballgown ballooning out behind her, revealing her bloomers.

Wolf looked down at her resignedly. "Ach, young women these days, Muthesius. They cannot take it anymore, eh? You would have thought that Le Petite Ecosse would have been different, having been suckled on whisky. Is that not what they say about the Scottish. Ah well, you better take her back to Hoffmann's. I'll make it all right with him tomorrow."

Muthesius helped Frances back up into a sitting position on the couch. "I'm afraid it will not be that simple," he said. "As I said, the lady's husband, accompanied by Herr Mackintosh, is at your gate. You must offer some explanation. The honour of our country is at stake."

What was it about patriotism being the last refuge of a scoundrel? Wolf hated the prospect of having to explain anything to the two foreigners, but he knew that it would not go well for him if Lueger found out he had besmirched the Government. Technically, Wolf held no high office, but everyone knew the power he wielded and many resented the fact. Plenty of influential people believed the man belonged back in the upstart Germany. He had not the finesse to serve such a fine, old and distinguished empire as Austria-Hungary. For once the man decided to let discretion be the better part of valour and sent his butler down to the gate with a message for the armed guards.

Muthesius sat beside Frances and mopped her brow with his handkerchief. He lifted the syringe case. "You didn't. . . . .?"

Wolf shook his head and replied with a sleazy grin "A pleasure postponed, perhaps"

Muthesius almost lost his cool at this. He really wanted to break Wolf's jaw, but just then MacNair burst in, completely sober now, followed closely by Mackintosh. Both rushed immediately to Frances.

"Fear not, my friends," said Muthesius, "she is sound asleep. Too much Champagne, perhaps. Let us make her more comfortable on the couch."

Instead, MacNair scooped his wife up into his arms. "No, she won't stay in this house another moment." He passed her into the arms of Mackintosh and marched up to Wolf.

"Explain yourself, sir. How is it that a man in such a high place can stoop so low as to abduct another man's wife? Speak sir, while you can."

Wolf sneered at him, his scar twisting. "A firebrand, eh? Forgive me, Herr MacNair, your red hair shows Pictish origins, perhaps, but you could not beat the Romans. It was left to we Germans to do that, no?"

MacNair slapped him hard across the face. "Scoundrel," he said. "I had expected at the very least an apology. I am at your service, sir. I demand satisfaction."

Wolf put a hand to his face. There was a thin trickle of blood on his bottom lip. "As you wish," he said. "Shall we proceed? These things are usually settled at dawn, but it is already well after midnight and my gardens are floodlit. I can furnish either pistols or swords, although I seem to be out of claymores."

Mackintosh and Muthesius looked at each other, both knowing that the situation had spiralled rapidly out of control.

He said to Wolf: "Don't be stupid, man. A duel? Those went out over a hundred years ago. Make this man the apology he is due and beg forgiveness from his wife. Be thankful that we may be prepared to let the matter drop without informing your superiors. I'd hazard that even you, Herr Wolf, are not above the law in this great city."

The German turned on him. "Ah yes, the great Charles Rennie Mackintosh. Master of art nouveau, king of the Glasgow Boys and darling of the youth of Munich and Vienna. Yet, there are those who say that your symbolism is morbid and your hellish rooms full of furniture better suited to a torture chamber. Some say that you are merely debauched.

"I happen to know that you own wife is more than captivated by that dirty little pornographer Klimt. But as far as the duel is concerned, it was your friend who suggested it, not I. I am merely defending myself."

Mackintosh lost his Highlander temper. "You are beneath contempt, sir. Name your weapon. I too demand satisfaction from you and I will have it first."

"Well, well," laughed Wolf. "I can die only once. Would it be too unsporting of me to suggest sabres, Herr Mackintosh? That would certainly give me an advantage since I see that you are, how shall I put it, not so mobile as most men. But then, in either of your cases, I really need no added advantage. How about if I take you both on at once. eh? Do you think that might even the odds?"

Muthesius could not believe what was happening and wracked with feelings of embarrassment and horror. "Have you all gone mad?," he said. "Charles, he is an expert with both sword and pistol. Two years ago he killed an Army officer . . . also over a woman. This kind of thing is meat and drink to men like him. You must rise above it. I implore you, don't fall into his trap. Right now you are reacting in just the way he wants you to."

He turned to Wolf. "Listen to me. These men are artists, not the bar-room brawlers you are used to mixing with. I urge you to make amends here."

Wolf retained his sneer. "But that is just the point, Herr Muthesius. They claim to be artists and are lauded as such, but are they not merely imposters, riding on the back of a talent and a movement which is essentially Germanic?"

Muthesius was struck then by a flash of inspiration. Suddenly he saw a way out of the mess so that none of three would lose face.

"All right, all right have your duel. But for God's sake let it be bloodless. Listen, the Darmstadt publisher Alex Koch . . . you know him Wolf. He is running a competition for the design of a large country house. He has called it A House For An Art Lover. The premise is the art should consist of the house itself, not necessarily in its contents. Already there are many young German and Austrian architects at work on the project. The deadline for the receipt of all plans is six weeks from now. Herr Mackintosh does not have much time, starting as he is, from scratch. Let your duel be fought within the parameters of this competition. Should Herr Mackintosh beat the Germans at their own game, you surely could no longer doubt the authenticity of his talent."

Wolf was already bored, but he saw that he had been out-maneuvred. Also, he had begun to sober up enough to realise that Mayor Lueger would take a very dim view of his behaviour and would probably get rid of him.

His eyes wandered to the syringe of drugs. He craved a shot of cocaine. Instead, he turned to the two Scotsmen.

Gentlemen. You have a very valuable ally in Herr Muthesius. You can see why we call him the Little Diplomat. Please accept my apologies. I fear that I lost my head. At the reception, you know, we were all a little drunk. Herr MacNair, I am an impulsive man. I was captivated by your wife's beauty. I may have been under the impression that you were not yet quite married. Forgive me, please. Herr Mackintosh.

"I beg you not to read any unsavoury implication on my part regarding your good wife and her attraction to Freud. Please forgive me. I have been under a strain. These are strenuous times to be working in foreign policy. Germany needs allies. The Russians and the French mean to crush us between them like a hen's egg in a vice. We must make friends with Great Britain."

The two Scots were far from mollified but they could see that the German was rambling. Such was the change in him that they both suspected they could be looking at a real schitzophreniac. The theories of Freud had not entirely gone over their heads. Wolf sank into an armchair with his head in his hands and the other three men were grateful of the opportunity to take their leave, MacNair carrying his still sleeping wife. It was almost two'o'clock in the morning. That afternoon, a procession of gifts, bouquets and letter of apology arrived for Frances at their rooms in Hoffmann's house, but she wasn't too put out when her husband binned the lot of them.

Their exhibit in the Secession hall was a great success. The various panels, friezes and distinctive pieces of furniture were the collective contribution of The Four, but gave the impression that only one talent had been at work. As well as the Waerndorfer music salon, the order books for Mackintosh furniture began to bulge. One critic wrote in the Vienna press: "There is a Christ-like mood in this interior. This chair might have belonged to St Francis of Assisi". In a separate section of the hall, the symbolist paintings of the MacNairs were also well-received, with many viewers murmuring that Klimt had competition. They went out to celebrate in a restaurant recommended by Hoffman, but it was just the four of them. They wanted to get away from the Austrians for a while.

Frances said to him. "But seriously, Tosh, you're surely not going to enter this House For An Art Lover competition. Wouldn't that be stooping to Wolf's own barbaric level in which everything has to be a contest?"

"No, Fran," he said. "Muthesius said he was going to tell us about it anyway so, you see, Wolf doesn't really come into the equation. I would have accepted Muthesius's invitation to enter.

"The competition has only recently been announced in the newspapers. The other architects have a head start on us only in the sense that they were anticipating it."

"Ah yes" said MacNair, "but don't they say that anticipation is nine-tenths of preparation."

"Who says that?" asked Mackintosh. "I think we'll have to put that down to a MacNairism. You've obviously been reading too much Oscar Wilde again."

Frances defended he husband. "Oh come on, as epigrams go it's pretty plausible. Well done, Herbie. You have just added to the English language and are therefore now a great man."

MacNair began to play the fool. He stood up, glass in hand. "Yes, yes I am a great man. And a brave one too. A toast my friends, to the Great MacNair, the Aubrey Beardsley of the North and stylist of our times."

The small commotion he had created attracted the attention of other diners, some of whom recognised them. There was a small ripple of applause and MacNair bowed theatrically. Frances was struck by a fit of giggling. Mackintosh, however, was in a more serious mood. He spoke to his wife.

"This competition is ideal for us. How many times do we baulk when prospective clients don't give us total control, or when they ask us to do only one room? This is another chance to design an entire house on a remit that specifies art. In Glasgow they are always saying me that I am more decoration than décor. Well, here is a chance for me to be expressive and also free. We will have cheated the Glasgow contradiction. We'll have a freer rein here than even for the Davidson house. We have to do it. Anyway I wouldn't give that bastard Wolf the satisfaction of seeing us pulling out."

"He was wrong about the Picts," said MacNair, apropos of nothing. The other three looked at him balefully.

"He said that the Picts could not defeat the Romans and that that job had to be left up to the Germans. But he missed the point. The Picts were not even trying to defeat the Romans. On the contrary, it was the other way round and the Romans failed miserably. Indeed, the Picts were the only race the Romans did not subdue and were so terrified of them that they had to build bloody big walls to keep them out of England. We Picts kicked their Roman arses right out of Britain"

"That's not true," said Mackintosh. "They had to withdraw their legions from Britain to go fight the Huns and Visigoths who were threatening Italy."

Margaret said. "Oh Tosh, would you really have fought a duel for me?"

"No, my love. I would have crept up behind him during the ten paces and tupped him a headbutt as he turned to fire."

This had MacNair in stitches. "Well, not exactly a bloodless solution, but certainly a Glasgow one."

****

They left Vienna on November 10, almost an entire month since they had set out from Glasgow. Telegrams had brought the required permissions for the extended stay. As upon their arrival, groups of students ran alongside their carriage calling and waving farewell, and eliciting promises to return for the Ninth Secession. During his many lectures to the students, his main theme was to convince them to be courageous and not be afraid of making mistakes. "There is hope in honest error," he said. "None in the icy perfections of the mere stylist."

At the station, they said their farewells to Hoffmann and Muthesius. Mackintosh had been working flat out on his designs for the House For An Art Lover and he now passed these, consisting of a portfolio of six scrolls, into Hoffmann's safekeeping. When the Austrian got back to his house he passed the portfolio to his butler, instructing him to lock it in the safe. As the servant made his way to the study, the front door bell rang. He placed the portfolio on a hall table and went to answer the door. It was one of the students, a young man from the university's arts magazine, asking to interview Hoffmann about the visit of The Four. The butler told the young man to wait while he went back to finish the job of locking up the Mackintosh plans. But when he got back to the hall table, the portfolio had gone.

CHAPTER ELEVEN

Strivers

The death of Queen Victoria on January 22, 1901, affected people in different ways but, whether they liked to admit it or not, everybody was certainly affected. There were those in their sixties who had never known anything else but the Victorian Age and the spread of Empire. For them, the effect was an unsettling fear. Life had been hard but they had always felt somehow protected by British expansionism. God knows what would happen under the dilettante Bertie. How much would the new king Edward VII try to meddle in Government?

To those still under forty years old, however, the death of the old queen came edged with a certain liberating quality. Certainly this was felt at 120 Mains Street in Glasgow, where the Mackintoshes laboured over the furniture and interiors for Windyhill.

"I think it best if I go and live with them for a while once they've moved in," he said to her. "Davidson has a charming family and the invitation is open. It will help me to get a real feel of the spirit of the place. Building a house is one thing but you have to live in it to allow it to speak to you."

"You talk about buildings as though they were human," she said. "But, of course, I know what you mean. A house can be dead or alive. Some people say when they look at your buildings they wonder if it is not the building looking at them."

He put down his pencil and took her in his arms. "Never forget that any credit I take for anything is down to you," he said. "We are as one. Did you know that the Austrians now refer to us as the Kunstpaar. The Art Couple. Certainly, Kate Cranston considers you to be a marvel."

The doorbell broke their clinch. Mackintosh went to answer it and returned with an opened letter in his hand. He had obviously read the gist it at the door and was in a blue rage. But, just as suddenly, he sat back in his chair and dissolved into gales of bitter laughter.

"It's from Muthesius in Munich," he said. "The results for House For An Art Lover competition have been announced. There were thirty-six entries but ours could not be considered because we failed to send three perspectives of the interior. For the rest, the judges were disappointed and awarded no first prize. The second prize has gone to Baillie Scott, an Englishman. Well, at least that's one in the eye for Max Wolf and his notions of German superiority. But look at this. . . . although we have not been considered, Alex Koch has published our drawings in a set of lithographed plates. Do you see what this means?"

"It means there has been some terrible mistake," she said. "Our plans were complete when we gave them to Hoffmann at the station. I checked, and all the interior perspectives were there."

"It means, my love, that but for the missing plan we would have won it."

"But what can have become of the missing plan," she asked.

"If it is sabotage," he said, "it has to be Wolf. Theft would have been the only way to do it, since Koch's people would have noticed immediately if any of the drawings had been tampered with."

"Oh Tosh," she said. "It's so unfair, It could have given you a real reputation throughout the whole of Europe."

He wasn't laughing anymore, but neither was he still angry. He took her in his arms again. "Don't fret. I will have other chances to establish my reputation. In any case, a European reputation would be worthless to me without one here at home and there is another competition coming up which is going to make me famous the length and breadth of this Sceptred Isle."

****

There were three morning commuter trains from Kilmacolm station to Glasgow Central . . . . at 6am, 8am and 9am. Local banter

86

said the first one was for the strivers, the poor folk struggling to make ends meet, the second for the thrivers, middle-class folk getting on in life, and the third for the drivers, the fat-cat bosses who had already made it. William Davidson, although very comfortably off now, certainly did not consider himself to be among the third category. He was a thriver still, and could not afford to ever let himself become complacent in matters of business. On this bright summer's day in July, a rarity for the West of Scotland in that particular month, the proud new owner of Windyhill, strolled along the Kilmacolm platform, glancing at the headlines in his newspaper and waiting for the transport he knew was never late.

His attention was distracted from the newsprint by what sounded like a snort of derision at his elbow and he turned to see Archie Lennox, an odious weasel of a man who had somehow managed to get himself elected captain of the golf club. Lennox was manager of a Glasgow bank and usually took this train, but he did not always give Davidson the time of day. . . . something for which the latter was almost always grateful. But apparently seeing no one more suitable for buttonholing that morning, the banker belligerently approached, waving his own newspaper.

The graceless little man in the ill-fitting bowler hat dispensed with the decency of formalities and immediately began braying at Davidson. "Will you look at this," he scraiked, thrusting his paper under Davidson's nose. "The Germans are building a bloody big navy a lot faster than we are turning out ships on Clydeside. Salisbury's spent all our defence money fighting the bloody Boers and that's just throwing good money after bad. This big German navy can only mean trouble, mark my words."

"And good morning to you too, Archie," said Davidson drily. "I must say I never took you for much of a patriot, the Boer War being a case in point. No doubt this lapse of investment on Clydeside is hitting your own pocket. Perhaps Lord Salisbury just disnae fancy your lending rates."

The wee man's face reddened. "I'm as patriotic as the next man, Davidson. And Germany's a lot closer to us than South Africa.

There's a big difference between battleships coming oot of the Kiel Canal and Dutch cowboys shooting at you with a rifle. Here, that wee gimpy fellow who built your hoose. Very friendly wi' the Germans, is he no'?"

Davidson knew then that Lennox had been manoeuvring towards this all along. The creation of Windyhill had caused some jealousy among the petty, and Kilmalcom had plenty of those. It was certainly bigger and grander than Lennox's house, which the man thought inappropriate since it was he, and not Davidson, who was the golf club captain.

Davidson said: "Charles Mackintosh staged a very successful interiors exhibition in Vienna last year, if that's what you mean by being friendly wi' the Germans. Being a brilliant and cosmopolitan architect doesn't necessarily make a man unpatriotic, Archie, if that's your implication."

Lennox was glad that Davidson appeared to have risen to his bait. "No, no. . . . just wondering why he hasn't exhibited anything in London, that's all, or even here in Scotland."

"Aye, well it could be that they are a bit more open-minded on the continent, Archie, and a wee bit more inclined to nurture and promote a budding talent."

Lennox turned vicious. "Maybe so, but it seems to me that it would take more of a *deranged* mind than an open one to build that hoose of yours, Bill. It's a blight on the hillside. My Moira says it looks mair like a prison or a barracks."

"Aye, and she should know." Davidson wished he hadn't said it but the man was beginning to annoy him. It had gone eight o'clock and he was wondering where the train was.

"Now look here. . . ", Lennox began, but Davidson had already walked away to the kiosk for matches.

They could see the smoke now from the approaching train and Davidson hoped that Lennox would board first so that he himself could sit away from him. Both travelled First Class. But the wee man wasn't about to let Davidson get away with insulting his wife to such a degree. He soon found Davidson's compartment as the train

88

pulled out of Kilmacolm on its twenty-mile journey to Glasgow, via Paisley.

It took about fifty-five minutes, having started from Greenock half-an-hour earlier. The train was busy but there was always plenty of room in the First Class carriage. Lennox stowed his bowler hat and briefcase on the rack and took a seat opposite his hapless acquaintance. There were two other men in the carriage but Lennox wasn't about to allow their presence to temper his language.

"I hear that your wee gimpy architect takes a bit of a bucket, Bill. That won't have done too much for the lines of your hoose."

Davidson ignored him and raised his paper, but Lennox persisted, warming to his theme. "And they say that booze is no' the only stimulant he's partial to. One of my girls was telling me about his country picnics at which the top item on the menu is opium. Him and eight weemin gambolling around the fields. . . is that natural? What they must get up to leaves nothing to the imagination, given those pornographic posters of his. Have you seen the one that advertised the Fine Arts Institute? A plain study in masturbation, if you ask me."

"Well Archie, it takes one to know one, isn't that what they say?"

Lennox looked apoplectic. "Are you calling me a tosser?"

"No, I've finished."

They were drawing dirty looks from the other two men in the carriage but Lennox wouldn't quit.

"It's not right for a man, particularly a man seeking professional reputation, to spend all his time in the company of women and Germans. . . and questionable women at that. The way some of them dress, and swan around with their hair down to their knees. I've even heard that some of them are suffragettes, including that wife of his."

"You say suffragette as if it were another word for child-murderer," said Davidson. "How can you condemn an adult woman fighting for the right to vote in her own country?"

Looking dreamily out of the window, as if mightily bored, he then played his trump card. "Ah well, I suppose all this antipathy towards Charles Mackintosh means there's no point in asking you and Moira round to Windyhill for tea. Shame really. I'll bet your

89

Moira would kill for a look at our new interiors . . . . that is, at Mr Mackintosh's interiors."

＊＊＊＊＊＊＊＊＊＊＊＊

Archie and Moira Lennox never did get to see the inside of Windyhill, but Charles and Margaret Mackintosh were guests of honour at the Davidson house one day during that year's festive season. Nineteen Hundred and One had been a good year for Mackintosh and he was happy to be the guest of one of the people who had made it so. He felt that he had at last become become recognised in his own city. The Herald and Daily Record buildings and the Queens Cross Church had been well received.

The new School of Art was attracting a lot of attention and work on the second phase was going well. The Cranston tearooms in Buchanan Street and Sauchiehall Street were packed with patrons drinking in both tea and the Mackintosh interiors. He had exhibited in London and Vienna and had been lauded in the most important trade magazines. The crowning glory had come when Keppie had offered to make him a full partner in the firm. He accepted, but it would be costly. He would have to pay his way in gradually but he felt the position fitted his growing status. At age thirty-three, he was not yet the architect he wanted to be, but he had one design in mind that would change all that and finally get him recognised in England. This of course, could open doors for him in all the countries of the British Empire, and even in the United States As Christmas approached, he was optimistic. They both were.

The drawing room at Windyhill was full of excited, laughing children, chasing and playing games, and dominated by the most enormous Christmas tree. Piles of wrapped presents were stacked at its base and its branches groaned with ornaments. But there were no Christmas-tree lights. It would be some years yet before stringed Christmas-tree lights became affordable and available to the mass market, so the Davidsons had lit their tree with candles in holders, which had been clipped on at strategic places. Mackintosh loved to play games with the children, his connection with them perhaps a little poignant, considering he knew he would never have any offspring of his own. And the children loved him back. Somehow his club foot and slight limp made him more accessible. They felt that he could never catch them in games of chase.

But when they caught him he was most generous and always came up with a silver shilling for a prize. It was decided that he would be Santa Claus and now he wore a big red-felt gown with hood and white cotton-wool beard, with his own natural moustache coloured white to match. He and Margaret had arranged coloured strings of wool around the room in a tangled maze. Each strand led to a written clue which if solved would reveal the whereabouts of a lovely gift. The children had to follow the strings. Santa Mackintosh then began to stack even more gifts from his sack to add to the pile under the tree.

The Davidsons had been serving aperitifs, but Mackintosh was far from drunk. However, to further delight the children, he could not resist trying to build a small house using the parcels as building bricks and failed to notice the proximity of his felt sleeve to one of the tree candles. His Santa gown went up like a Chinese lantern, bringing a scream from Margaret and footsteps in the passageway as Davidson came running. By the time he got there Mackintosh was a ball of flame but his host kept a cool head and, lifting a seltzer syphon, sprayed his guest until the fire was extinguished. There was nothing left of the cotton-wool beard and Mackintosh's own moustache and eyebrows had been singed but, apart from that, he was unharmed. But when they laid him down on the chaise longue to properly check him over, he seemed to have gone into mild shock and took some minutes to fully come out of it.

As Davidson handed him a brandy, he raised himself slightly from the couch and whispered in the ear of his host: "Fire, William. I have a mortal dread of it."

CHAPTER TWELVE

The Cathedral

"The walls of your fortress are going to collapse unless you buttress them up," he told her.

Frances was down on the shore making an ornate sandcastle, using Lindisfarne as her model. The Four had come to Holy Island again, a favourite retreat of theirs off the coast of Northumberland, on a short summer sketching holiday. Mackintosh was particularly keen to see what his hero Sir Edwin Lutyens had done to Lindisfarne Castle (circa 1550), having just refurbished it for the wealthy publisher Edward Hudson. The key was to make the place more habitable without impinging on any of its Gothic splendour. Mackintosh intended Gothic splendour to feature largely in his next project.

Frances sat down in the sand beside him and stole a look at what he was drawing, then gazed up the hill at the real castle. "Do you really think it kept out the Vikings, Tosh?"

"A castle is only stone and iron," he said. "The only thing that can really stop a determined man is a more determined man. Castles and forts are just so much apparatus ---- of practical importance of course, but without the power to break a man's spirit. I think the Vikings would have got in if they had really wanted to, but in any case it is a moot point since the castle wasn't there during Viking times."

She blushed. "Oh yes I forgot. It was the monastery the Vikings attacked. But would the monks not have had God on their side? Wouldn't He save them?"

"Not necessarily. A man cannot save himself, or his soul, by becoming a monk anymore than he can by building a cathedral."

His sudden reference to a cathedral startled her, but then the truth slowly dawned and she began to realise why he was taking so long to sketch the castle. She stood up, brushing sand from the back of her skirt.

"Why, Tosh. I do believe you are going for Liverpool."

He stopped sketching and looked up at her. "Yes, and as a full partner. The entry for the new Anglican Cathedral at Liverpool will be submitted by Honeyman, Keppie and Mackintosh. This time I'll be able to claim the design as my own. This is the one I've been waiting for."

She became perplexed and her vexation surprised him. Like her sister, she was usually so supportive of all his endeavours.

"Oh Tosh, I wish you wouldn't. I couldn't bear to see you disappointed. Liverpool is an open competition and will attract every Tom, Dick and Harry. Couldn't you be more selective?"

He stood up and pocketed his sketchbook. He sensed straight away there was something she wasn't telling him. She and MacNair had lived in Liverpool for more than two years now and their lives centred around the university, which was pioneering the architectural degree. It was a radical move. Until now, no one had a hope of ever becoming an architect unless they could somehow gain an apprenticeship with a firm or buy their way in.

"What do you mean you couldn't bear to see me disappointed?" he asked. "What makes you think I will be?"

She became tearful and turned away from him to face the sea. The movement of her shoulders told him that she was sobbing.

"My dear girl, what can be the matter? I've never seen you so upset." He put an arm around her. "Let's go back to the cottage and get to the bottom of this."

"No, no please," she said. "I don't want to see the others just yet. I don't want Herbie to see me like this. He has worked so hard. Oh I feel so foolish. This sounds awful, but I've missed you both so much since we went to Liverpool. It's a horrible place. I'd give anything if only we could be back together at the old art school, working together again as The Four. We have been damn near ostracised since Herbert took that university post. I fear that our scant

93

reputation preceded us somewhat and they want nothing to do with us. The English laugh at us and regard us as freaks."

"There must be something we can do," he said. "Is Herbert applying for other posts?"

She shook her head and accepted his handkerchief. "It was Herbie who overheard them talking. His boss, Professor Simpson, and the London architect Charles Reilly. Reilly hates anything to do with arts and crafts... hates the Victorian Neo Gothic. Reilly himself has entered the competition with a classical design , but he was telling Professor Simpson he did not expect to even get beyond the first stage. The word in London, he said, was that the King himself had remarked how wonderful and appropriate it would be if the winner turned out to be the young Giles Gilbert-Scott. Apparently, King Edward is a great admirer of George Gilbert-Scott, Giles' late grandfather. The old man was, of course, responsible for the Albert Memorial, for the King's father, and a paradigm of the Gothic revival. Salisbury Cathedral is his, St Pancras Station, St Mary's Cathedral in Glasgow. The King always gets what he wants, Tosh. But Herbie says they have to go through with the competition anyway because it has been announced.

Mackintosh was stunned. He kept staring out to sea as though expecting the tides of fate to rise up in a tsunami and drown him.

"Giles Gilbert-Scott," he mouthed the name. "But he's only a boy. What has he done?"

She took his hand and they walked away, heads down, along the shore, leaving the tide to consume Frances' now semi-collapsed sandcastle of Lindisfarne.

****

"When were you going to tell me about it?" They were back in the bar of The Corinthian again and he handed MacNair his pint.

"Oh come on Tosh. It was only the third opportunity since the Reformation to build a cathedral in England. The Sassenachs were always going to keep that one to themselves."

"But Giles Gilbert-Scott, for Christ's sake. The only one of his designs that was ever realised was for a fucking pipe rack"

The Corinthian still furnished spittoons at regular intervals along the footrail but his profanity drew a frown from an aproned bartender.

They supped in silence for a minute. MacNair said: "The profession DID advise against submitting anything Gothic. . . . "

"Balderdash," he interrupted. "It had to be Gothic. The last great Gothic cathedral ever. And I had to be the man who built it. A crossing tower, two lesser towers, the flying buttresses. . . . "

"Sounds like a trapeze act," MacNair re-interruped. "Those buttresses would have done for you anyway, Tosh. Certainly, the chief assessor Bodley was against them and he had all the clout. Let me read you his written decision, in case you've forgotten what it was."

He fished in his pocketbook for the relevant envelope and extracted a folded sheet of paper. He spread it out on the bar in front of them.

"The Mackintosh buttresses," he read, "with those friezes of figure sculpture in between, would have put immense weight on the aisles and deprived the clerestory windows of light".

"But that's outrageous," Mackintosh was becoming loud in his indignance. "Light is my main material. Light is what I fashion first before I even look at the three-dimensional. A blind man can see that in everything I've done. Did Bodley not look at the measurements, for Christ's sake? The distance between those buttresses is enough to let through roomfuls of light, and the white stone sculptures and marble plinths would have reflected it. Those bastards just stuck their heads in the sand."

MacNair lit a cigarette. "They also said, off the record, that your design was somewhat over-grandiose. They knew about the restraints forced upon you with the School of Art. They considered that your design for Liverpool was perhaps a reaction against this, that this time you were trying to make sure the beancounters would have no excuse to fragment your work. As a result, they feel you may have overdone it. . . "

"How can you overdo a fucking cathedral?" he roared. "Not just any cathedral, mind you, but the last and greatest Gothic monument

95

in Britain. Bentley's Westminster has put them to shame. Didn't they want me to outdo the fucking Catholics?"

This time the tough-looking barkeep with the white apron and slicked-down hair walked over and told him to mind his language, but he was already finishing his pint and heading for the revolving doors.

"See you later Herbie," he said. I have to go and give a lecture on Seemliness to the spotty-faced students at the uni. Have a good trip back to Scouserville and give my love to Frances. See you both at the end of term. . . "

"As well he left before I threw him oot," said the barman. "No need for that kind of language, is there sir?"

MacNair stood up and stuck out his neck aggressively. "Every need, John," he said. "Every fucking need."

****

He stood behind a lectern in the lecture hall, perspiring in the stuffy heat of this bland, windowless amphitheatre, and perhaps a little bit drunk. The twin ironies did not escape him; he had come to talk about decorous, good taste and the building he was standing in had been designed by George Gilbert-Scott.

There wasn't much of an audience, with most of the students away for the summer and only certain departments remaining open for revision. Many of those who had turned up were actually studying civil engineering. Some of the students at the front caught a whiff of the drink on him and there were general smirks and catty comments. They were all men, apart from one attractive young woman.

"Good afternoon gentleman . . . . . oh and lady. Ah, you may smoke, but no drinking. Those addicts among you who cannot do without a dram may be able to absorb one through osmosis simply by sitting nearer to me."

There was a ripple of laughter. He had, at least, successfully broken the ice.

"Well, I don't know why you are not all off to Tuscany or Florence or somewhere similar that your professors have told you

you're supposed to be at this time of year. . . . though I can tell you that such sabbaticals did nothing for me when I was a student, except fleece me of what little money I possessed and get me a painful dose of the pox."

If he was anticipating a look of reprimand from the young woman, it never came.

"Anyway, since you are good enough, or earnest enough, to be here in what is technically the holiday season, I propose to dispense with the formality of the course notes. While I'm at it, I might as well also dispense with the lecture on Seemliness, ha ha. But far from wasting your time , my friends, for I am sure you are more than adept at doing that without my assistance, I want to talk to you about something which, in the end, may be the only thing that matters, and that, my young friends, is freedom."

They sat in silence, intrigued by this small , charismatic man with a limp and rather in awe of his Spook School reputation. At that point, Mackintosh's jovial air began to dissipate and his voice took on an emotional quality. He spoke with a deal more gravitas.

"Freedom as any African-American slave will tell you, as any Russian Jew or Irish Republican, or even any common British working man will tell you, comes at a very high price. It is a price so high that it is often never attained, so that most people live and die under the iron heel of oppression . . .social, economic, religious or otherwise. But I don't want to turn this into a political lecture. The kind of freedom that you, as the builders of tomorrow, need to strive for if you want to make your mark in any way, is the freedom of spirit required to go it alone and to break off the shackles of tradition and authority. In art, and in life, my friends, it is only the advocates of individuality, freedom of thought and of personal expression who succeed in taking mankind farther along the road of civilisation."

The young woman stood up. "You say freedom has a high price, Mr Mackintosh. So freedom is never free?" Another ripple of laughter. "What will be the price of freedom for us should we choose it?"

He turned to give her his full attention. "Nothing but more oppression," he said. "Oppression in its many horrible forms . . . . punishment, exclusion, ostracisation, loneliness, perhaps even insanity. Take courage, my dear. You must be independent, independent, independent. Shake off all the props, the props that tradition and authority offer you. Go alone. . . . .crawl, stumble, stagger, but go alone. . ."

"Preposterous rubbish," came a shout from the back. "Are you telling us to court insanity, Mr Mackintosh?"

The speaker was a tall young man with red hair, egged on by three of his rowdier friends. "Where's the freedom in being a lunatic or an outcast? Oh yes, we'd be free all right. Free from our minds, free from any prospect of employment . . . "

A wave of fatigue hit Mackintosh and he stumbled at the lectern, looking as if he were about to fall over. Some of the young men at the front moved forward to assist him but he quickly regained his balance with protestations that he was quite all right and just needed some fresh air. The lecture on Seemliness, it seemed, had ended in a most unseemly manner.

The students filed out. There had been no applause. Mackintosh followed them, fishing in his pockets for a small cigar. As he walked towards the exit he caught sight of a small man in a business suit and bowler hat, taking notes. As he drew nearer, the man quickly rose and scurried out of the theatre. Mackintosh didn't think he was one of the students, but he did think he had seen the man somewhere before.

CHAPTER THIRTEEN

Mansions Of Glory

The students' hostile response to his lecture didn't bother him much but he took a walk through Bellahouston Park to clear his head and consider whether he should temper any such talks he might be required to deliver in future. He had slept late and would not go into the office until after lunch. It was a hot sunny day and he walked with his sleeves rolled up and his jacket over his arm. Scotland was actually having a few days of summer. He took a tram back to Bath Street feeling a ood deal better about his general disposition, but was instantly dismayed when Mary, the secretary, told him his presence was required in Keppie's office. He found his new full-partner to be ostentatiously amiable. It did not suit the man, he thought, just making him appear silly. He was immediately suspicious.

"Sit down, Charles, there's a good fellow. A drink perhaps? I've a new case of fine malt."

Keppie made to go for it but Mackintosh declined. Drinkers ARE particular about with whom they imbibe.

"Forgive me for saying so Charles but you seem, how shall I put it, a trifle distracted of late. That Liverpool Cathedral job was always going to put us on the periphery, you know. I wouldn't let it get me down."

He looked balefully at Keppie and for an instant toyed with the idea of telling him the truth -- about the express wishes of Good King Bertie, the revered George Gilbert-Scott, his spotty-faced little grandson Giles and the Great English Establishment. But suddenly, he couldn't be bothered.

"Of course, John," he said. "Why give such an important national and iconic monument to a provincial architect, eh? In any case, the Anglicans probably couldn't have stomached their new cathedral being created by Scottish Presbyterians. They probably think we're all heathens up here."

Keppie relaxed a little, believeing that Mackintosh was starting to get over the whole disappointment.

"Aye," he laughed, "Apart from our immigrant Irish papists. The Anglicans are scared of them."

This comment illicited no response whatsoever, so Keppie pressed on.

"Look, Charles, I've something here that might help you to move on from this Liverpool business -- a building no less important than a cathedral, in fact some would say more important."

Keppie lit his pipe. Mackintosh continued to stare glassily into the middle distance.

"It's another school. After all, you are a full partner in the firm now and we all know what a fine job you made of the Martyrs School building back in ninety-six. And, Charles, I think you'll like it, offering as it does, a lot more scope for your creativity. I think you'll agree when you examine the remit."

Mackintosh still said nothing, but he fished for a small cigar.

"The governors was us to design the new Scotland Street School for the Glasgow Board -- a much larger commission than the Martyrs. I thought you might like to come up with some sketch plans. Ah, here's the remit."

Keppie proffered a briefcase. Mackintosh stared at it for a few moments before reaching out and taking it. Finally, he spoke, but when he did his voice sounded so dead and emotionless that Keppie thought he must be choking on his cigar.

"Yes, John," he croaked. "Of course. The Scotland Street School. It will be an honour … a privilege."

Mackintosh picked up the briefcase and headed for the door, but Keppie quickly came after him.

"I don't mean to pry, Charles, but if there's something bothering you and I can help in any way . . . the both of you seem so miserable."

"Both, John? What do you mean?"

100

"Jessie, Charles. You and Jessie. You never ask for her. You never even inquired why she left her part-time job here. She did love it so."

Mackintosh looked at his colleague as if he were mad. Could it be that the man still entertained hopes of a reconciliation between his sister and Mackintosh? Did he not know that he was talking to a married man of almost two years -- and a very happily married man?

Mackintosh opened the door and walked out, leaving Keppie looking sad-eyed and puzzled. But Keppie then seemed to come to and, following his partner out into the corridor, called after him:

"JJ has heard all about your lecture on Seemliness. You've been taken off the list."

****

The remit he carried in his briefcase for the Scotland Street School had yet to inspire him, but he couldn't bear to examine it in his office, albeit that he had been upgraded to a far more spacious suite of rooms. He took the remit for a walk. He couldn't find MacNair in any of their usual haunts and wondered if the two of them had gone back to Liverpool, so he decided on the relative peace and quiet of the cocktail bar in the Central Hotel on Gordon Street.

He liked the Central Hotel building for its freedom of expression. Designed by the Edinburgh architect Robert Rowand Anderson, it had opened only eighteen years previously and was a wonderful and successive blend of both the classical and the gothic. But he despised cocktails and ordered a whisky and soda. At the bar, he heard a familiar voice from behind him.

"Never too early for a livener, eh Tosh? So, are long liquid lunch hours one of the perks of becoming a full-time partner?"

The banter was delivered by Talwin Morris, a young and sympatico friend of The Four who, at the tender age of twenty-five, had risen to the position of art director at the Glasgow publisher Blackie & Son. The young man looked prosperous and Mackintosh had always enjoyed his boyish enthusiasm. He also liked what Morris was putting on the covers of Walter Blackie's books. His mystical, Celtic-dreaming designs paid much homage to those of Margaret's own.

"My God, Tosh, do buck up. You look as though you've just been to see your tax inspector."

"No, Keppie."

"Oh Christ, same difference. Do forgive me."

"Forgiven. What's an aesthetic perfectionist like you doing in this halfway house for commercial travellers and loose women? Haven't gone Bohemian have you?"

"No, Tosh, not yet anyway. In actual fact, I followed you in here. I was across the street and saw you go through the revolving doors."

"Yes, well I can't stay for a session, Talwin, I've a new job on and . . ."

"How about making it two jobs?" Morris interjected. "Come over to the Press Club. There's someone there I want you to meet."

"Could it be one of your literary chums, Talwin? Conan-Doyle, perhaps, or maybe even Oscar Wilde?"

No, neither. And to tell you the truth I've started to feel I've stuck my neck out a bit on this one. It's the bossman himself, Walter Blackie. He wants an architect to build him a house -- not just A house but THE house -- so I recommended you."

Mackintosh had a new school under his arm but he was getting fed up of schools. This fact made him feel slightly guilty, as if he were withholding his obligations to his vocation and to society to satisfy his own selfishness. Still smarting from the cathedral rejection, he longed for the curious mix of tranquillity and excitement that designing another big house would bring him.

"Does the great Mr Blackie know that I demand total control?"

"Not yet," said Morris, and they headed for Argyll Street.

Walter Blackie wheeled from the fireplace, port glass in hand. A tall, dark man, he was, at age forty-nine, still in possession of a fine head of black hair under wich he cultivated a small, clipped moustache. He was very lithe for a man hitting fifty, very much a Victorian and very rich, but not stuffy or patrician in the Victorian sense. The new century had instilled in him the genuine desire to be

102

modernist, progressive, liberal, good to his children and grandchildren and sympathetic to the arts.

"I've bought land at Helensburgh," he told Mackintosh, "near where I want to sail my yacht. I dislike red-tiled roofs, especially in the West of Scotland with its frequently murky sky."

"The Ballachullish slate quarries," said Mackintosh.

"I beg you pardon"

"The Ballachullish slate quarries, that's where we'll go for your roof. Their product is a wonderful shade of dark blue. Oh, by the way, do you know William Davidson? I recently built a house for him at Kilmacolm."

"Only by reputation, sir. The City, you know . . . "

"Yes, well I think you had better come with me to Windyhill."

DESIGN BY DESIRE

PART TWO

CHAPTER FOURTEEN

Pressure Of Work

In the spring of 1906 they moved out of their tenement flat in Mains Street and bought a three-storey house in Florentine Terrace in the West End. He paid £975 up front. They transplanted much of the astonishing Mains Street interiors, but here, with more space, they were able to create symphonies of light and shade, with a startling white drawing room and more muted tones for the dining room and bedrooms. The Japanese influence was more evident in this new home.

He was doing well. Walter Blackie had been delighted by Hill House at Helensburgh and the Scotland Street School was generally considered to be a remarkable achievement. Now he was working on another house. At age thirty-eight he found that houses were what he preferred. They set him free. In his younger days there had been the twinge of conscience that if he were not designing a utility then he was making no contribution to society. But he was mellowing. Perhaps it was time to start doing things for himself for a change -- for Margaret.

The new house was Auchinibert at Killearn, for Francis Shand, assistant manager of the Nobel explosives company. MacNair had told him it was a dynamite commission. He hadn't laughed. He was also working on more tearoom interiors for Kate Cranston, the latest in Ingram Street. It was a fertile period and, as if to underscore his growing reputation, he was, in March, summoned by the governors of the Glasgow School of Art and told that he could expect a most encouraging development.

Alarm bells rang, but he chided himself for his cynicism. The Building Committee was headed by Burnet and also contained the leading architects William Salmon and David Barclay. He should at least show willing, but he was nevertheless glad to be accompanied to the city chambers by Francis Newbery, who was also on the committee.

105

The men who had created Glasgow sat in front of him at a long table. He felt a little bit like Judas might have felt at the Last Supper, though he wasn't really sure why. Burnet opened the proceedings by directly addressing him.

"I am sure you will be delighted to learn, Mr Mackintosh, that we have decided that now is the time to go ahead with Phase Two of the new Glasgow School of Art. But I have to tell you, sir, that there is no question of going ahead with your original design."

Mackintosh said nothing so Burnet pressed ahead. "I will hand over now to Mr Barclay."

Barclay was stocky man in early middle age, who seemed to growl behind his big mutton-chop grey whskers. He was Deacon of the Incorporation of Masons and the designer of more than forty schools, including Glasgow Academy. Mackintosh knew that the word "decorative" was not in the man's vocabulary. Barclay leaned forward.

"It is the unanimous view of the governors and the board, sir, that the new phase of the art school be constructed under more practical considerations. Fire safety requires more than one staircase. The task, sir, that we have all agreed upon, is to complete the Renfrew Street range, add a third tier of studios, design a whole new west wing and put staircases at either end of the building."

Mackintosh fished for a small cigar. Barclay stood up and looked down at him as if handing out some great favour.

"Honeyman, Keppie and Mackintosh, sir, will be appointed architects for the Second Phase. You yourself will continue as the project architect on the strict understanding , the strict understanding, sir, that neither you nor your firm are at liberty to instruct any extra work or alterations to plans without the written authority of this committee. You will note, sir, that a matter of over-spending on the Scotland Street School has still to be fully resolved. We require sketch plans, Mr Mackintosh, by the middle of next month."

Mackintosh finally broke his silence "Of course, gentlemen. The middle of next month."

But he knew that with all the pressure of his other work it was going to be a struggle. That night he worked at the office into the wee, small hours and on until dawn. At 7am, old Murdoch found him asleep at a desk strewn with papers and an empty bottle of whisky in the bin at his feet

****

Mackintosh's dynamite commission, as described by Herbert MacNair, almost blew up in his face. In the two years since he had sat in front of the art school building committee, Mackintosh had fought tooth-and - nail with the man Shand and his eccentric wife over the construction of Auchinibert.

They were Manx. It became clear that they didn't really know what exactly it was they wanted in a country pile situated between Loch Lomond and the Campsie Fells. Towards the end of the project, Mackintosh's site visits tended to consist more and more of a quick return to the bar of the nearby Crown Inn, where he had taken a room. And it was here that he sat, in the bone-dissolving cold of a Scottish February, in the year nineteen-hundred-and-eight, scanning the missive that had been forwarded to him by Margaret.

It was a letter from the art school building committee and he thought it enough to drive any man to drink. The letter protested unauthorised and extravagant works on the sub-basement porch and entrance and objected that the library gallery in front of the windows would reduce light and serve little purpose.

It was early afternoon and he felt the effects of two pints already downed. There was no one else in the bar and he had read the letter out loud to the barman.

"You see the kind of penny-pinching shite I have to put up with, Alistair. I'm no' exactly the Tsar of Russia trying to double the national debt to put a new extension on the Winter Palace."

He ordered another pint.

"I told them I could make savings later. New plans for the library will be very expensive. The basement porch is nearly finished. Do they want me to tear it down?

" The barman. Alistair, a red-headed man in his early fifties, presented him with his third pint.

"Ah don't know much aboot buildings," he said, "but ah know a piece of work when ah see it."

He was looking over Mackintosh's shoulder towards the lounge bar entrance. Mackintosh turned on his stool to see his wife walking towards him. She said only four words. "it's your father, Tosh . . . "

****

The completed Charles Rennie Mackintosh Glasgow School of Art was formally opened on December 15, 1909. This time, he decided to turn up. He sensed that he had created something special and that the creation was bigger than the sum of all its parts. It was a sensation shared by those who had always believed in him.

Speeches were being given in the main hall and he sat , cocooned in warmth, surrounded by those people . . ..Margaret, Frances and Herbert, Fra Newbery and his daughter Mary, Talwin Morriis, William Davidson, Walter Blackie, Kate Cranston and Hermann Muthesius. The guest speaker was none other than Sir John Stirling-Maxwell, a tall and handsome man in his early forties, 10th Baronet of Pollok, philanthropist, and patron of the arts.

It was clear that Sir John himself did not quite know what to make of the building and, even among the school's own students, opinion was divided among those who found it challenging and exciting an those who considered it too much of a mishmash of art nouveau and practical construction.

Stirling-Maxwell's end-of-speech presentation of Mackintosh perhaps reflected this:

"I give you then, the new Glasgow School of Art, and its creator Mr Charles Rennie Mackintosh, a man who will deserve well of his generation if it is only because he has made them think . . . " (sic)

Mackintosh tore up his prepared response. His spontaneous reply brought nervous giggles from the students and frowns of exasperation from Keppie, Burnet and Barclay. Margaret almost burst out laughing.

He said: "Far be it from me to assume the role of an instigator of thought processes in others. A presumptious thing for any man to do, I should think, unless those others are completely brain-dead. In that case, of course, it becomes an act of mercy, a way of saving themselves from themselves, if you will. Yet such a man risks a lot, my friends, for while he will be investing much of himself in the

108

resuscitation of the zombie, that poor creature itself may give him absolutely nothing in return . . . not even the civility of a simple thank-you."

The party in the main hall that night brought back memories of Vienna. The Mackintoshes waltzed to the small orchestra, surrounded by well-wishers who stopped to offer many congratulations. This was what Margaret had always wanted. She knew that they still had a long way to go, but this very special evening seemed to indicate that at last they were well on their way.

Life for Tosh, it seemed, had begun at forty-one. But she was in for another surprise. They left the dance hall and he brought two cups of punch into one of the studios where they could sit in comparative seclusion.

"You never looked more beautiful," he said to her. "Looking at you in these surroundings, it's as if you belong here. So much of this place is you, not me."

She laughed: "All of this place is you, Tosh, though I'm happy to be credited with providing a little of your inspiration, knowing, as I do, that it is based on our love."

"Then this place is built on love," he said. "What a charming notion, though try telling that to those old buzzards at the top table."

She laughed some more: "You were a little hard them today, Tosh. Your speech barely disguised your contempt. Do you know that you actually called them a bunch of brain-dead philistines, although in that clever way you have of delivering insults by the back-door. It was perhaps injudicious, especially when you know how important they are to the wellbeing of the firm."

He drained his punch cup and gripped her shoulders.

"Bugger them. That doesn't matter anymore … the firm, I mean. I'm sick of Keppie and his constant thinly-veiled allusions to Jessie and I'm sick of having to work constantly hounded by accountants and other people who have no appreciation of what I am trying to achieve. I can hardly cope with all my own private commissions as it is, never mind the firm's. It's time to move on."

"What are you saying, Tosh?"

"I'm saying that I quit. Tomorrow I resign my partnership from Honeyman, Keppie and Mackintosh and start out on my own."

CHAPTER FIFTEEN

Adrift

In the event, he did not tender his resignation to the firm until more than three years later. She had pleaded with him and, as always, he had acquiesced. It was just as well. If he had been riding the crest of a wave at the opening of the completed new art school, he was now drowning in the doldrums. The signs had been there as early as January 1910. The new art school had caused sufficient reaction in Glasgow itself for the firm to have it glamorously photographed by Williams, one of the top London photographic houses, hoping that this might lead to spreads in the trade magazines up and down the country. But no interest was shown.

In 1911, the work coming into the firm halved, and in 1912 it halved again. He was drinking heavily. He had been trying to keep himself busy with additions to Kate Cranston's Ingram Street tearooms and had even stooped to a hairdressing salon which the owner constantly complained of. But then at the end of that year a competition was announced for a large and important project --- a teacher training college at Jordanhill. However, for the first time in his career, he failed to make the sketch-plans deadline and the job was taken away from him. By the following June, he decided that his position in the firm had become quite untenable. It began to feel embarrassing for him to go to the office and so he finally did quit. In the straitened circumstances of the times, Keppie accepted his letter.

He opened up on his own in a small office in Scott Street, but no work came his way. Were the Glasgow freemason patricians deliberately freezing him out, feeling that they had little enough to keep themselves occupied? Or was it just a sign of the times? Probably both. His profession had moved on. The signature architect and the cult of the decorative, it seemed, were now things of the past --- in Britain at least.

The Mackintoshes survived by making furniture, retaining the good business of previous private patrons, especially Kate Cranston. Walter Blackie also stayed faithful and it was on a dreich October day in 1913 that Blackie himself called in at Mackintosh's dingy office, ostensibly to chase up some pieces for the Hill House.

The place looked like a tip and, despite the gloomy day, the shutters were drawn. Blackie found Mackintosh sitting alone with a half-empty bottle of whisky on his desk. The great architect was bedraggled, unshaven and surrounded by hundreds of sheets of paper on which various drawings of various imaginary projects had been sketched. They spilled on to the floor and overflowed in the bins. Blackie saw right away that the proprietor was drunk.

"Are you all right, man? Margaret asked me to call round. She's worried. What on earth is this you've been doing."

Mackintosh squinted at his visitor through his lazy eye.

"Did you know that when Talwin Morris died his family asked me to design his tombstone? He was only forty-five, you know, and quite beautiful."

"But what of the living, Charles? How are you keepi9ng, man?"

"Not keeping at all, really. Might as well be dead myself. Who do you think would design my tombstone? Charles fuckin Reilly perhaps."

He opened a drawer and threw a folder at Blackie.

"The new college of domestic science . . . the Dough School. It would have put me back on my feet, you know. It would have saved the business. But I know that I'll never get anymore work in Glasgow now. Listen to this:"

He took a sheet of paper from the folder and began to read: "We regret the unsuitability of your plans as the wash-hand basins are on the wrong side of the corridor".

111

Blackie declined the offer of a dram, so Mackintosh helped himself.

"I had plenty of work when I resigned from Keppie, you know. Small jobs, yes, but with the promise of bigger things to come. However, as soon as I set out on my own, the work dried up. How could that be, do you think? "

He drained his glass and poured another.

"It was very hard, Walter, to receive no general recognition. Only a very few see any merit in my work and the many pass me by. Even the very students attending my art Glasgow School of Art have called the place bizarre. It is hard for a man of my age to think that he has wasted all of his time in the wrong place."

Blackie pulled up a chair and sat down opposite his troubled friend.

"But you are still young, Charles, certainly on the age scale of architects. You cannot expect universal recognition having been born in the wrong country. You are certainly right up there with the best in Europe and better than Gaudi."

Mackintosh was touched to even have been compared to the great Catalan builder of Barcelona's spectacular Sagrada Familia and allowed himself a wan smile.

"You are a beautiful man, Walter. I am happy to have built you a beautiful house."

He corked the whisky bottle and dumped it in a filing cabinet.

" Come on, let's get out of here. It never was a place of business anyway and it's time to shut it down."

"But what will you do now?" Blackie asked.

"Margaret suggests a holiday. We haven't had a proper one in ten years. But, of course, I cannot pay for it. Fra Newbery has offered us his cottage in Suffolk for as long as we like. Friends have always been so kind to us."

"Not at all, man," said Blackie. "What small things people give to you they give in return for the amazing, unique and irreplaceable things which you give to them. But I think you know that. Come with me now, I'll take you in the horseless carriage. Margaret is waiting for you."

He put on his hat and coat and followed Blackie out into the hall. But before turning out the lights he went back and retrieved the whisky from the cabinet drawer.

****

He was drunk in a pub somewhere near the Trongate, far from the comparative salubriousness of the Old Corinthian Bar. The office whisky had tipped him over the edge and he hadn't wanted to go to the Corinthian under the influence. Fellow professionals knew him there and he still had his pride.

This dive was a dark place. Rods of dust-moted sunlight battled with the big heavy wooden shutters, while a pair of huge-bladed roof fans tried to cut the bad air and tobacco fug. He became dimly aware of unsavoury characters lurking in corners, of a skeletal young woman begging pennies for gin -- despite a large sign behind the bar which read NO IRISH, NO BEGGARS AND NO CREDIT.

It had been a while since he had seen MacNair and he knew that his friend was in trouble. Things had suddenly gone badly for them In Liverpool and they had come home to Glasgow looking to start again. Margaret had gone to see Frances, offering help and a roof should they be in need of one. Frances had been relieved to come back but MacNair was ashamed.

He ordered another pint from the filthy-aproned barman behind a horseshoe counter that, despite the sparsity of patrons, was strewn with dirty glasses. Next to the big mirror there was a cosh on a hook. He drained his pint past the halfway mark and held the glass up for one of the sunlight rods to penetrate.

"A singularly unremarkable design, my good man, so functional as to be almost brutal. Pray, tell me, who is your supplier? Surely not one of the Venetian houses, eh?"

It took a few moments for the barman, a small man with a cut across his right cheek that looked as if it hadn't quite healed, to realise that he was being addressed. When he did, he was less than amused, given he hadn't a clue what the drunk customer was on about.

113

"Whit's the matter, a bad pint? You should have said something before now. It's nearly finished. . . you and it baith, if you ask me."

"A bad pint? Certainly not, my dear fellow. A bad receptacle perhaps. But the refreshment you purvey is never bad, only the cause of the thirst that craves it."

The barman was having none of it and looked as though he was about to eject Mackintosh for taking the piss at his expense. Besides he would have been justified in ejecting a drunk person. Mackintosh sensed the aggression and, desperate not to be thrown out, he placed two half-crowns on the counter and invited the barman to take a drink and to serve the others in the pub. He soon found himself surrounded by assorted beggars, tramps and the gin woman. He wondered if they meant to mug him outside. A man with a sooty face, though he probably wasn't a chimney sweep, came in through the swing doors with a collie dog at his heels. The dog urinated in the sawdust. No one said a word about it. Suddenly Mackintosh did not feel drunk anymore, just very sad. He began to speak, to no one in particular.

"Look at this place," he said. "I tried to make Arcadia in the Underworld but when I look at you people I see it was hopeless from the start. You are people made ugly by an ugly place. This city is ruled by ugly men who want to keep it as ugly as themselves. Hear the ugly names they have given to its districts. What must the outsider imagine these places to be like? It is the meanness of ruthless commerce, whose prosperity is only the joyless ostentation of a Shylock. . . a dark and dying thing. I sought the truth in beauty but beauty here is regarded as frippery and altruism as foolishness. You poor wretches will always be poor because of the oppressive policies of the brutal capitalists who use you . . . who allow you a pittance for drink to keep you down, dull and stupid. Cheap wine and laudanum. Glasgow's opium is the opium of the British Empire . . ."

The motley crew around him retreated back to their corners. They were afraid of madmen. The monologue had finally convinced the barman to throw him out, but Mackintosh was already heading for the door. He turned to deliver a parting shot.

114

"I curse this city. Let it always be ugly. Let it never rise above the bestial. Let it ever be divided in its petty religious bigotries. Let it wallow in the grime of its greed and fester in the poison of its dark, satanic mills. Let it wither in the small-mindedness and pedantry of its fathers."

He made it through the swing doors just in time, for the man with the sooty face, flushed with that kind of strange civic pride which is so incongruous in the underclass, picked up Mackintosh's empty pint glass and hurled it after him. It smashed against the inward- swinging door and all hell broke loose as the Great Unwashed scrammeled for the five shillings and the barman with the weeping cut unhooked the cosh.

CHAPTER SIXTEEN

I, Spy

By the day of his eleventh birthday, young John Lowe had already read Baden-Powell's book on reconnaissance twice and had won all the scouting badges --- the youngest in his patrol to do so. His one big regret in life was that he had been born just a handful of years too late to join the Suffolk regiment now fighting in northern France. Well, if he couldn't fight the Germans in Europe, he could damn well do his best to do it in England and the splendid brass telescope his dad had given him for his birthday would take pride of place among his armory of catapult, sheath knife and compass.

With the Great War just a month old, young John was already on a mission. For nearly a week now he had been closely watching the movements of the stranger on the shore. His mother had said the man was an artist who had arrived with his wife to take up residence at Millside Cottage. The parish of Walberswick attracted artists and in high summer might be said to have a colony.

John Lowe wasn't so sure about this man being an artist. He didn't look like one and, for a start, where was his easel and palette? But, more importantly, why did he spend so much time down on the shore, gazing out to sea. . . . gazing over to Holland? And young John knew his quarry wasn't an Englishman. He had been in the village shop when the man bought cigars. He had never heard a Scottish accent before and had thought it sounded very Teutonic. In the few weeks since the war had begun, vigilance was the watchword for those not fighting overseas. But eleven-year-old John Lowe, too young to join the Suffolks, was planning to contribute a bit more than vigilance to his own private war effort.

However, if the Scouts had a stealth badge, young John might have had to give his back. Mackintosh knew the lad was following him. Mackintosh was forty-six now and there remained practically none of the dashing cavalier. He had filled out more and shaved off his moustache. His hair had thinned and turned an almost girlish light brown. Margaret thought it suited him, making him look a lot less fierce and reflecting more accurately his gentle soul. Another major change was that, after nearly half a century of defying his birth defect, he now got around with the aid of a walking stick. It was indispensible to him, for walking was, these days, high among his pleasures.

And here he was again, walking on the Suffolk shore. Despite the heat of the late August day, he wore a frock coat and deerstalker hat with earflaps. John Lowe watched him drink from a bottle he had produced from his coat pocket.

Probably schnapps, the boy said to himself, adjusting his telescope for a stronger focus.

John watched on as the man began to walk towards the sea, letting the waves wash over his shoes and the turnups of his trousers.

Queer fish, he thought. Is he going to commit suicide? No, more likely try to signal to a Hun submarine. John had read all about the new German U-Boats.

He put down his telescope and took from his haversack the cheese sandwiches his mother had made him for lunch. He had bought some lemonade from the village shop. He ate quickly and mechanically, not really savouring his repast, anxious to keep tabs on the stranger on the shore. But he was too late. When he picked up his spyglass again the man had gone. Still, he couldn't have got far. A sandy path ran up from the shore to the village outskirts and John decided he would go down and follow it. The footprints were easy to trace. When he got to the gate at the top of the path, the man was leaning on it and smoking a small cigar, as if waiting for him to arrive. He used his walking stick to point at the boy's belt.

"A fine knife you have there. I always wanted one when I was your age, but would never have been allowed it where I come from. You must be a good and sensible lad to be trusted with such a blade."

John had no trouble understanding the man, but still thought the musical lilt in his voice to be very strange. He was also a little annoyed at having been so easily confronted by quarry he was meant to be stalking and decided there was no point now in continuing with the subterfuge.

"Are you a German spy," he said boldly. "My father is in the Coastguard and he told me to be on the lookout for suspicious characters."

The man suddenly abandoned his air of friendliness and turned on his heel, marching away in the direction of the village as fast as his limp would allow.

Even the local pub seemed bent on surveillance. The village inn was called the Hereward The Wake and the landlord's name was George Barclay. Mackintosh was encouraged by the Scottishness of the name , but quickly disabused. The man was a supercilious prick, happy to take his money for a double whisky while quietly disapproving of such heavy drinking so early in the day. The Newberys, Francis and Jessie, had been holidaying here every summer for some years, so Barclay knew all about the artists at Millside cottage.

But he wasn't so sure about this new couple. And when his postmistress sister told him the Mackintoshes were receiving letters from Germany, the shocking revelation sat maliciously in the man's suspicious nature.

Barclay served the large dram. "Found anything to inspire you, sir?" he asked. "For painting I mean. You don't seem to carry any materials down here."

"He thought I was a German spy," blurted Mackintosh. "For Christ's sake. What I have built is not for the Kaiser to destroy."

Barclay somehow found himself disappointed that Mackintosh had cut straight to the chase by bringing up the subject of espionage. It seemed less likely now that he really could be spy, but perhaps the man with the strange gruff accent was trying to pull off a double bluff.

"Who called you a German spy, sir?"

"Who . . . what? Oh, just a boy. A boy with a spyglass, not finding what he was hoping for but believing it just the same."

Barclay mopped the counter. "Well, you know what these youngsters are like, sir. Since the war started their imaginations have been running riot. Suspicious of everyone they are, and if you ask me it's no bad thing. We all have to be vigilant in these times, sir. You never know who might be walking among us."

Mackintosh drained his glass and the whisky made him playful. He decided to have some fun at "John Bull" Barclay's expense.

"Quite so. But there's a difference between being vigilant and being a vigilante. Unfortunately, the Germans are our enemies now, but they are still a great and cultured nation from whom we can learn much. It works two ways, of course. For example, did you know that in Munich I am considered a hero."

He had gone too far.

"I wouldn't mention that to anyone else around here if I were you, Mr Mackintosh. There are people from Munich trying to destroy us. Perhaps you should go there if you are so popular with the spikeheads."

"I'd go if I could," he said. "But it's impossible because of the war. The worst of it is that neither can I do anything here because of the government moratorium on all new building. And so I paint my watercolours and I drink my liquor and I pray for a private commission. I do not, as it appears is becoming the generally held notion around here, spy for Germany. Good day to you, sir. Spikeheads indeed"

The first thing he saw when he got back to Millside was the military car parked on the grass verge outside the gate. Margaret, who had been watching for his return, came running down the garden path in a state of some agitation.

"Oh Tosh, be quick please. They're wrecking the place. They've cracked my cheval mirror."

A soldier was guarding the door. An officer was sitting at the kitchen table while two other privates and a sergeant completed their search of Millside, including the outhouse the Newbery's had given the Mackintoshes to use as a studio.

When Margaret came into the kitchen Mackintosh noticed blood on her cheek. He lunged at the officer, but the sergeant , on his way back from the barn, intercepted and manhandled Mackintosh on to the floor before detaining him at pistol-point.

"You bloody oaf," shouted Margaret. "This man is an artist and he's not been well. What do you mean by roughing him up?"

The officer said: "All right Jenkins, that's enough. Help him on to the couch."

The officer, a captain in his mid-fifties, seemed very bored and world-weary and looked as if he wished he were somewhere else.

"My name is Worth, madam. I'd really like to get through this without anymore unpleasantness. It may have escaped your attention, madam, although I doubt it, but the behaviour of your husband here has been causing no small alarm to the people of this parish. . .. late-night walks by the shore, gazing out to sea, certain unpatriotic opinions expressed in the village shop. Then, of course, there is his accent. Scotch it may be, but many of the villagers have never heard anything like it. And now there's this . . "

He produced from a breast pocket an envelope addressed to Mackintosh and carrying a Vienna postmark. He took out the pages and held the letter at arm's length as if it were a piece of ordure.

"From the Kunstfruends of Vienna, madam, whatever they may be. Addressed to your husband here and acknowledging him as their master."

Margaret watched Jenkins's face redden.

"You see, madam, this is enough to convince my sergeant here. I dread to think what would happen to you both if some of the rougher and, how shall I put it, less educated elements of this parish ever saw this letter."

She was fearless in the face of the veiled threat. "You bloody ignoramus," she hissed. "The Kunstbund is a group of Austrian artists and designers with whom my husband has been corresponding for years. They don't cease to be out friends just because of this stupid war."

120

Captain Worth shook his head sardonically. "Tut, tut, madam. Stupid is it? That's not very patriotic, is it? I wouldn't repeat that outside of this cottage. . . not unless you want to be taken for a coward ----- or a communist. And as for the Austrians being your friends, well that's as may be. They may privately be your friends but, officially, I'm afraid they are in fact your enemies. Given, of course, that you are British."

Mackintosh got shakily to his feet. "Don't be preposterous man, of course we're British. I'll have you busted to corporal for this. Where's your search warrant? I'll sue you and your bloody commanding officer."

Now Worth stood up and confronted Mackintosh, almost nose to nose. "I shouldn't go making any more trouble. We haven't found any communications equipment here, but if we'd had then you'd both be in very hot water indeed, and so would the Newberys. As it is, I'm taking you in for more questioning. Your wife can stay here in the meantime. I'm not so much of an oaf and ignoramus as to maltreat a lady. Her small cut was unfortunate, a tiny shard of wood from the mirror-frame when Jenkins knocked it over."

"You can't take him way," pleaded Margaret. "He hasn't been well. Please, let him alone. We are quite prepared to move away from here."

Worth turned to face her. "I am sorry, madam, but I have a duty to perform. These are sensitive times and the people here are afraid. They are afraid of what might be dropping out of the sky or what might be emerging out of the sea. They are afraid of strangers who stay too long and who exhibit behaviour which some might call eccentric. When they are afraid they can be dangerous. Your husband had better come with us, madam, for his own safety."

They drove him to the police station, which had one small cell, and locked him up in it. In the evening they brought him ham and eggs and a mug of tea. In the morning, the duty constable could hardly believe his eyes when he went to check on the prisoner. Mackintosh had covered all four walls of the cell in pencil drawings . . . designs for pieces of furniture and buildings he would never be

121

commissioned to make. Others showed copies of houses and interiors he had created in the past. The cell had become a vast cubic mosaic.

At 9am he was visited by Captain Worth. The duty constable opened the cell door.

"Very impressive, Mr Mackintosh. Very impressive indeed. Of course, you'll have to wash it all off."

"Are you referring to the walls, captain, or to the inside of my head?"

Worth lingered. Looking at the drawings with a more intense gaze. Mackintosh began to identify certain pieces for him, telling him where they were, when he had made them and for whom.

Worth took off his officer's cap and sat on the bunk. "My son was training to be an architect," he said. "Now he's in Belgium blowing things up. How bloody ironic."

Mackintosh asked him for a smoke and accepted a Capstan cigarette.

"Remiss of the bobbies not to have searched you properly. Still. I'm willing to accept that you are what you say you are and that you may indeed be a brilliant man. But that's not going to make one whit of difference to the simple people of this insular little parish. We've checked out all your letters and they seem genuine enough. You can pick them up at the desk on your way out of here. Once you leave the police station my advice to you is to keep on going. You and your good lady should find somewhere to work away from here. . . . away from the English coasts altogether. Why don't you go home, back to Glasgow?"

Mackintosh gave a snort of derision and crushed his cigarette underfoot.

"I think I'd rather stay in this cell for the rest of my life than go back to Glasgow. Now if you'll be good enough to supply me with a bucket and wire brush I'll restore this bijou interior to a chamber fit for a criminal."

Worth stood up and again examined the drawings.

"Is that a writing desk? My word, sir, can't say I've ever seen anything like it. And this dining-room suite. Looks like something from the palace of the Emperor of China. This stuff must be for a rich man's house."

"Or a house for an art lover."

When he walked out of the jail into the sunny mid-morning she was waiting for him and they embraced for a long time.

"So they no longer think you're a German spy then, Tosh?"

"Damn it, Margaret, I'm as patriotic as the next Glasgow drunk."

"The last refuge of a scoundrel," she laughed, but the mention of Glasgow made her wistful. She had loved working in her studio there before they had sold up.

"Well, we can't stay here and I refuse to go home. For the first time I'm scared. What's to become of us, Margaret?"

"Never mind," she told him. "No man is a prophet in his own back yard."

"And in my case, it seems, not in anyone else's back yard either, eh?

They walked back to Millside. Across the flat fields they could see the chuffing smoke from a locomotive pulling six carriages on the coastal line. The train was on its way south . . . on its way to London.

CHAPTER SEVENTEEN

Model Client

The train came thundering out of the tunnel travelling much too fast. The track curved sharply into a viaduct close up ahead and the steam locomotive couldn't hold the bend. The four rear carriages slewed to the right and disconnected from the three at the front, tumbling over the sheer drop of the mountain pass to the floor of the valley below. The rest of the train shot through the viaduct but failed to make the outer turn and went hurtling off the track and into the air . . . . only to land on a large, soft velvet cushion.

"The viaduct's too close to the tunnel," said Wenman Bassett-Lowke.

It was an elaborate layout that wound its way through rolling hills, a farm, a polished-glass river and even a small village. Bassett-Lowke stuck his face between two papier-mache mountains and peered down at the track like some Greek god on Olympus.

"Perhaps another two carriages."

"Who is this wee fellow standing at the station?" inquired Charles Rennie Mackintosh, pointing to a three-inch figure made of lead that sported a long white beard and bowler hat.

"Could be anybody, I suppose", said Bassett-Lowke, "but I modelled him on Bernard Shaw. I thought it might amuse the great man. We've become quite close friends ever since I joined the Fabian Society."

Mackintosh had heard of Shaw. His father being from Cavan, he had always retained an interest in all things Irish, especially the question of independence. He knew that Shaw's hit play Pygmalion was still running in the west end. But he wasn't sure that he cared too much for the Irishman's politics. Mackintosh was working class, but of the conservative variety, not the socialist kind. He feared the rising power of communism and thought socialism to be a watered-down version of it. Events in Russia one year's hence would reinforce his fears.

It was the autumn of 1916 and the Mackintoshes had taken lease of two studios next door to each other in Glebe Place, Chelsea. They were living on Margaret's small inheritance and what they could make from fabric design. When Bassett-Lowke commissioned Mackintosh to modernise the big Georgian house he had bought in Northampton for himself and his bride-to-be, it had come as a Godsend. They needed the money and the 39-year-old Basset-Lowke had plenty of that. His model railway business was famous throughout the land and he grown even richer through the war contracts won by his engineering company.

His wife loved the Northampton house, which was called Derngate. But Bassett-Lowke couldn't stand the idea of living in rooms that contained anything older than he was. He decided the house required a complete makeover. He had been unable to find an English designer willing to work in the modernist style but, on holiday in Cornwall, he had met a fellow engineer from Glasgow who had recommended Mackintosh.

Mackintosh now stood in Basset-Lowke's London warehouse, watching the man playing trains. Perhaps the Englishman's vast wealth has given him something of a guilty conscience, he thought. The Fabian Society indeed.

At age forty-eight, Mackintosh, looked a good bit older than the man who had stalked the shores of Walberswick. His hair was going grey and his face had now thinned out. He had developed a reddening of the nose, the spidery blood vessels betraying his continuing fondness for whisky. His lazy eye had almost closed and his limp had become more pronounced.

Bassett-Lowke noticed this and was quick to suggest more comfortable surroundings.

"My dear Mr Mackintosh, thank-you so much for coming. But perhaps you'd prefer it if we adjourned to my London house. It is not far."

125

Mackintosh hated it when anybody sympathised over his disability. Besides, he was still enjoying the trains layout. "No, no this will do splendidly, sir. Where better to discuss grand design than amidst perfection in miniature?

He limped c loser to the layout and examined it with a completely genuine enthusiasm. He hoped Bassett-Lowke would not think he was being patronised.

"A truly beautiful achievement, sir, and all the work of one man. There is no design by committee here, am I right?"

Bassett-Lowke was flattered in spite of himself. "You are too kind, Mr Mackintosh. It is a little hobby of mine which I have managed to turn into a business, but I prefer to think of it, not as a profitable enterprise, but as a way of supplying my fellow enthusiasts at affordable prices. I will not produce a piece for which a schoolboy cannot save with a few weeks' pocket money."

"Anything that brings a little diversion to anyone in these dark times is to be welcomed, is it not?"

"Quite so. But tell me Mr Mackintosh, what made you agree to take on Derngate? I fear it may not be worthy of your talents being, as it is, a humble terraced house and one of no great dimensions. Indeed, you might even call it small."

For a fleeting moment, Mackintosh thought about playing the prima-donna with the man. It might mean a higher fee. But just as quickly he decided to be perfectly frank and honest.

"These are lean times for architects. The government won't let us build anything due to the war and there is precious little in England left to design. But you said in your letter that this house is for your wife-to-be and it is surely this which has captured my imagination. We can collaborate, sir, but I must tell you now that I have to have a free hand. This must be impressed upon your good lady as a condition of my accepting the commission. The size of the house is immaterial to me. Rest assured that I am used to having to perform miracles in confined spaces."

He bent to examine the train layout again, chuckling at its charm, making the small leaded figure of George Bernard Shaw shuffle along the platform.

****

126

George Bernard Shaw was shuffling along the platform. Dressed in a cream linen suit with waistcoat, he carried a small carpet bag and walking stick --- one of which seemed to aid his progress while the other hindered it. The long white beard underneath his homburg hat made him unmistakable but, arriving at Northampton first class from London, he had been so far unaccosted. Public fan worship was, in 1917, thankfully still a phenomenon of a few decades hence.

The great man, sixty-one years old now, was on his way to the house-warming, and Bassett-Lowke had sent a car. He had not yet decided whether he would spend the weekend at Derngate and was not really sure why he had agreed to go in the first place. He thought Basset-Lowke a most agreeable and entertaining fellow, but he really didn't DO housewarmings. It was the name Charles Rennie Mackintosh that had swung it for him. Shaw had seen the catalogues and his curiosity was piqued. Besides, it would be fun to go into an Englishman's "castle" in the company of another Celt.

In just under a year, the Mackintoshes had transformed Derngate and the Bassett-Lowkes were delighted. Now Wenman was as excited as a child at Christmas at the prospect of two great men meeting under his new roof.

The theatre had given Shaw a keen interest in interiors and, after the grand tour, conducted by Helen Bassett-Lowke, the great man was effusive in his praise. Shaw had lived in London for more than forty years but still spoke as one could imagine a leprechaun might --- a strong Dublin accent delivered in a thin, piping voice.

"Remarkable, Mr Mackintosh, truly remarkable. A place of magical contrasts . . . of light and dark. . . of masculinity and femininity. There are rooms so white and cool they remind me of the Mediterranean. And my own bedroom, a singular arrangement of black-and-white chequerwork, a veritable dreamscape just waiting for its grateful and weary occupant."

Mackintosh, not yet drunk, was determined to stay modest and gracious.

"Some might call that room nightmarish," Mr Shaw. I trust the harshness of the lines will not disturb your sleep."

"Oh I very much doubt it. You see, I always try to make a point of sleeping with my eyes closed."

Margaret liked that, despite it being at her husband's expense. She said: "It is unusual to find such good humour in a man who is called a literary genius, Mr Shaw. Are not such men usually so serious?"

"You mean like your husband, Mrs Mackintosh?"

She blushed.

Mackintosh was quick to support her. "Forgive me, Mr Shaw, but Margaret is the genius of this partnership. I possess only talent."

Florence Bassett-Lowke brought sherry and petit-fours. "We have not found Mr Mackintosh stern in any way, Mr Shaw, if that's what you mean. Serious about his work perhaps. Thorough, yes, and pristine to a fault. But all in all, a most agreeable companion and collaborator. You have heard otherwise?"

"No, no," said Shaw. "Serious about his reputation, as all men should be. I have been told that during his time in Suffolk Mr Mackintosh was accused of spying for the Germans and detained overnight in a police cell. He has taken great pains, badgering the authorities in London to clear his name."

He turned to Mackintosh. "I confess that is how I first heard your name before I studied your work."

"Think nothing of it, Mr Shaw. It is true that I have many German friends, but I hope I am as patriotic as the next man, if not more so. But what about yourself, Mr Shaw? You must have strong feelings about what is happening in your own country. There are young men dying in Ireland's struggle to be free just as there are on the mudfields of France."

"Of course, I have strong feelings about Ireland," he said. "But they're not necessarily patriotic. Patriotism is a pernicious, psychopathic form of idiocy. It is your conviction that your country is superior to all others just because you were born in it."

"You don't really believe that, do you?" Margaret asked him.

"Ireland's struggle is economic, Mrs Mackintosh, just as England's is imperial. Everything could be settled through negotiation if mankind were not so barbaric. Our impulse to

128

slaughter each other is primeval and innate and patriotism is one of the excuses. It is the beast in us that we must transcend."

The man's apparent contempt for patriotism riled Margaret, who had been particularly affected by enormity of the losses in Belgium and France.

"Is that what socialists believe, Mr Shaw, or cowards?"

This stopped everyone in their tracks and the company fell into a sudden, tangible silence. But Shaw was not offended.

"Please, madam, do not be so quick to bestow your white feather. I can assure you that in this day and age it takes just as much courage to speak the truth as one sees it than to run screaming out of a trench and offer oneself up for butcher meat. It takes brave man to stay sane when insanity surrounds him."

Florence said: "You speak of the beast that we must transcend, Mr Shaw. Is this beast perhaps the devil?"

"I have no doubt of it, dear lady, if the devil is but another term for all the evil in the world."

"Really Mr Shaw, you surprise me," interjected Margaret. "You sound almost religious. Do not socialists like yourself believe that religion is the opium of the people?"

Shaw was warming to her, despite her apparent determination to test him.

"That is a Marxist epigram, Mrs Mackintosh, and a good one. But Marx applies it to communism, which is altogether another form of madness. You have been following events in Russia?"

"Of course, and I have also read Marx. His idea that the history of human civilisation has been but a history of class struggle intrigues me. Was not his revolution supposed to happen in this country, since we were the first to industrialise?"

"Clearly he thought so," said Shaw, "but I could have told him otherwise. You see, we have something in this country that will always keep the lower classes down . . . an obstacle that the Russian revolutionaries won't have to overcome."

"What can that be?" asked Florence.

"Our language, dear lady, and the way in which we emit it. There can be no unity here, no rising of the proletariat, when it is impossible for one Englishman to open his mouth without making another Englishman despise him."

"Oh you mean like Eliza Doolittle, and Professor Higgins?" said Florence. "But they fell in love . . ."

"Does this apply to Scots as well?" asked Mackintosh.

"Yes it does. Any man in this country who sees himself as a revolutionary leader would do better to see about shortening the alphabet than the working hours of a factory wage slave."

Margaret got in fast. "Why how preposterous. What on earth can you mean by that, Mr Shaw?"

"Simply, dear lady, that the seemingly arbitrary relationship between the Roman alphabet's letters and the English language's sounds contributes to the general malaise. No man can teach himself what the English language should sound like from reading it."

"I think I'm still with you," said Mackintosh. "But how would a shortening of the alphabet help?"

"A phonetically-based alphabet would be shorter. It would enable us to dispose of a good many of those redundant letters which serve only to confuse."

Bassett-Lowke backed up his friend. "The idea being," he said to Margaret, "that through such methods as shortening the alphabet, social reform can gradually be brought about, rather than by bloody, violent revolution. This is a core belief of our Fabian Society."

Margaret could not disguise her smirk. "Could then social reform also be helped by more agreeable interior decoration? Perhaps, Tosh, you are an unwitting Rousseau."

A maid entered with a tea tray, but Mackintosh wanted something stronger. He hinted to Bassett-Lowke that perhaps Shaw could also use a drink after his journey. The playwright twigged right away.

"My father had a drink problem ---- and a squint," he said. "I often wondered if the latter was caused by the former, or vice-versa. I thought he was winking at me all the time which, of course, made for a riotous state of affairs when was WAS winking at me. God knows what he must have looked like to the chorus girls at The Gaeity, for he either winked or squinted at them all the time."

Mackintosh burst out laughing in spite of himself, for he had been shocked by Shaw's implication.

"You forgot to mention my limps, Mr Shaw. Or could it be that you have not yet had enough time to see me walking. It is more of a problem, as you call it, than the drink."

"I think not, Mr Mackintosh. Forgive me if I speak out of turn, but I have seen in this house what you are capable of. Your limp, sir, may eventually destroy your hip, but whisky will almost certainly destroy your soul."

The two of them had adjourned to the garden and the maid had brought them a decanter,

"My soul is already destroyed. Torn asunder by masters."

"But your work. You are a man of no small reputation among architects . . ."

Mackintosh drained his glass and poured himself another double. Shaw declined.

"Exactly, sir. I am a man of no small reputation among architects and no large reputation among architects. I have no reputation among architects other than being a bloody German spy, as you so kindly pointed out. You say I have a reputation. Can you name anything of mine? Have you been in any of my buildings?"

"I cannot claim to have had that pleasure but . . ."

Mackintosh drained and refilled again. "Well, you are in this house, aren't you? Modernise, my arse. I practically rebuilt it for them. And you have visited, have you not, the Anglican Cathedral at Liverpool?"

"I understood that to be the work of Gibert-Scott, the er, younger one . . ."

"It is mine, sir. I tell you it is mine, yet no credit do I receive. They stole my design and then told me I had failed to reach the second stage of the competition. Gilbert-Scott was told to radically alter his original submission and my blueprints were plundered."

"Of course, the trouble with competitions," said Shaw, " is that one is completely at the mercy of the scoundrels who devise them. By charging entry fees, they make a killing at both ends."

"A cynical view, Mr Shaw. Many professional men, certainly architects as I have striven to be, rely on competitions."

131

Shaw accepted a small dram. "Forgive me, Mr Mackintosh, but the power of accurate observation is commonly called cynicism by those who do not possess it."

There was a silence, not uncomfortable, in which Mackintosh smoked one of his cheroots while Shaw examined the garden.

Presently, Mackintosh said: "You know, that's a load of horseshit you wrote about any man becoming a success if he really wants it. What if the bastards who pull all the strings won't let you?"

Shaw sat beside him and looked into his eyes. "You must take the bastards, as you call them, out of the equation. Go to the people. That's what I have had to do with my plays. That's what Bassett-Lowke has done with his trains."

CHAPTER EIGHTEEN

Frances

How could they have fallen so far? Looking back on it all now, she realised that all she had ever wanted was for The Four to be reunited in Liverpool. The early years of the new century had been so promising, with the move from Glasgow, the birth of their son, Sylvan, and MacNair teaching at the School of Architecture and Applied Art. Liverpool University was taking a new approach, seeking to create new architects through degree courses rather than by the traditional and hitherto only way in through the purchase of expensive apprenticeships. They had exhibited interiors in both Vienna and Turin and life seemed full of promise.

They had been in Liverpool only a few years when the competition for the city's new Anglican cathedral had been announced. Her heart had soared. Charles' design was so brilliant it was bound to be accepted and it would make his name. Charles and Margaret would be able to get out of Glasgow at last and The Four would be reunited.

But she had reckoned without Charles Reilly.

She almost laughed when she recalled the man's appearance. With his round, pockmarked face, black cloak and trademark fedora he actually looked like the pantomime villain.

But the cathedral competition assessors did not laugh when Reilly submitted his own design for what was to be one of the most iconic structures in England and, indeed in the whole Empire. George Frederick Bodley and Norman Shaw were in agreement that the cathedral had to be gothic. But Reilly loathed all Victorian neo-gothic and art nouveau and the man's reputation was growing. He was the son of the architect and surveyor Charles Reilly senior and had forged a strong following in London with his love of practical classicism and, in particular, the American influence. Having just failed to gain the professorship at University College, London, he came to Liverpool highly recommended. He was adored by his students. He detested Mackintosh and all he stood for and felt more than vindicated when even the students at the Glasgow School of Art had called the place bizarre.

But what was truly bizarre, thought Frances, was that the inexperienced rookie Giles Gilbert-Scott had won. How had that happened? Well, the new King had dropped a strong hint, and the young man's design, though shambolic, was at least gothic. Charles Rennie Mackintosh had never had a look in.

Charles Reilly's classical entry did not make the second stage, but the man was not so easily got rid of. His popularity among the students and his pioneering influence in establishing a way into the profession through a university degree rather than an exclusive apprenticeship had seen his star rise higher.

He was regarded as the coming thing, the new broom that would once and for all sweep away stifling Victoriana. In 1904 he was offered the Roscoe Professorship of Architecture at Liverpool. In 1905, he sacked Herbert MacNair.

It had been the week before their little boy Sylvan's fifth birthday. Frances had never imagined that being sacked from a job could affect a man so badly.

MacNair had simply seemed to crumple into nothing. Always a drinker, he now became a drunk. The wee boy looked so much like his father and MacNair had doted on the child, but now he began to neglect him. Frances' work suffered. She began to feel she was now wet-nurse to two babies. MacNair became depressed. She had soldiered on for three more years while MacNair found whatever work he could, but it was always menial. Soon they would not be able to afford to keep on their house in Oxford Street. Surely things could only get better.

Things did not get better. MacNair had always drawn a small stipend from his well-off family, which had done well in property and coal-mining. It had suddenly been withdrawn. Then came the letter informing them the family business was bankrupt.

By the spring of 1909 they were back in Glasgow but there had been no retrograde reunion of The Four. Somehow, things had not quite seemed the same. Margaret had offered whatever help she could and was glad of the opportunity to get to know her nephew, who was growing to be tall and strong. But he was a reserved and quiet boy who showed no artistic aptitude. They saw that Mackintosh himself had grown somewhat cynical, if not bitter. After the opening of the Glasgow School of Art Phase Two, their meetings became fewer. MacNair could not resurrect whatever it was he had had in Glasgow. In 1913 he went to Canada, leaving Frances behind with the boy and the tender mercies of her elderly parents. But in the New World, all MacNair could get was factory work and at the turn of 1914 he was back in Glasgow. There had been few meetings of The Four before the Mackintoshes left that summer for Walberswick.

Between 1914 and 1921 they had moved home five times. MacNair had started and aborted several disastrous business ventures, dragging Sylvan in to assist, blunting the boy's confidence with each new failure. Their apartments had become smaller and smaller and she now found herself, at the age of forty-eight, in a two- room flat in a rundown tenement in a bad street in the East End. She had spent the last of what she had putting all her work in storage. There were hundreds of paintings.

In four days it would be Christmas, but MacNair and Sylvan, now a strapping twenty-year-old man himself, had been gone for more than a fortnight, trying to establish yet another new business venture somewhere in Stirlingshire. She wondered if they would be back by Christmas Eve. She had not been able to afford to buy them any presents.

One framed portrait was not in storage and now she took it from her bottom drawer and set it on the cheap camping table in front of a hearth fire which had collapsed to glowing embers. It was a freezing night but she did not put on more coal. She had become so estranged from MacNair and had hated him for his drunkenness and for his abandonment of his vocation. If truth be told, she had not much loved her son. But now she studied the portrait. Now she felt the regret.

She poured gin into a half-pint pub tumbler and began talking to the picture.

"Where are you now, my darling? Wandering and itinerant for want of a family. Where are you now, my love? I could have given you so much more. I have loved you for so long."

She drained her gin glass and poured another. She made her way unsteadily to the wardrobe and returned with her carpet bag, rummaging in it to extract a small paper-wrap of powders. She poured the contents into her gin glass.

"Too late now, my darling. Wherever you are, I cannot follow. Wherever you are not, is a miserable place."

She drained the glass and lay down on the couch, her long hair, untainted by any grey, falling around her face.

"Poor Herbert," she said.

They did not come back on Christmas Eve, but at noon the following day. MacNair was surprised to see, propped on a cheap camp table beside the body of his dead wife, Annan's portrait picture of the young Charles Rennie Mackintosh.

CHAPTER NINETEEN

Friends In Need

Derngate put him back on the map for a few years, but it didn't last and none of the architectural commissions he won in London came to fruition. Fickle clients, legal problems and bad planning. He insisted on total design but few potential clients were willing to give him such a free hand. They worked on at the Glebe Place studios, living in the apartments above and producing prints for textiles. But it didn't pay very much and, by the winter of 1922, their situation had become desperate.

His studio was an empty shell, unheated, and lit on this dark December day only by a bare, dirty bulb that flickered. They were dressed in winter woollens, each with long scarves. Margaret attempted to boil water for tea on an old Bunsen. Mackintosh told her he'd stolen some sugar lumps from the Blue Cockatoo, the nearby restaurant where they took their single daily meal. The restaurant was popular with the Chelsea Bohemian set of artists and musicians. The sugar lumps were in a pocket of Mackintosh's only good coat, which he kept for dining out and which he would not wear while working, but it had been so cold the previous day he had put it on under his overalls. It was now on a hanger on a peg by the door.

As Margaret rummaged for the sugar, an envelope fell out of one of side pockets. It was unsealed and contained no letter but it had been addressed in Mackintosh's familiar hand. It was to William Davidson at Windyhill. It had been a long time since she had thought about Glasgow and what they had left behind there. She was about to ask him what it was all about but he intercepted her.

"The letter is in the other pocket," he said. "I wanted to let you see it before I posted it. You know that and grammar and spelling are not my strong suit."

She fished out the letter, a single sheet, and unfolded it. She read:

137

"Dear William, I find myself at the moment very hard up and I was wondering if you could see your way to buy one of my flower pictures or landscapes for £20 or £30. I am just about to start some work that will bring me a fair remuneration. I shall be glad to hear from you within the week as my rent of £16 is overdue and I must pay or leave".

Her face reddened under her auburn hair. She was aflame.

"For God's sake, Tosh, what is this? I know we are at a low ebb but this is nothing more than a begging letter. Mr Davidson may have been a friend to us some years gone, but to beg of him now? How will I ever live this down? I could not even bury my own poor sister without my mother's help and she has been left with practically nothing. And now here we are, going cap-in-hand again."

"Your search for sugar has yielded something less than sweet," he said. "But I have been corresponding with William these past few months . He is that true friend, the friend in need."

"Corresponding? Is that what you call it? So he has already given you money. But what about my allowance . . . and the designs we sell."

"Not enough, Margaret. The designs market is saturated. They pay pennies. Your allowance keeps us fed and something of a roof over our heads. But London rents are high and the Government has been after me for unpaid taxes. Listen, Margaret. It is not so bad as you paint it. I am not begging from Davidson. He is a collector and I am offering him originals. Anything he lends over and above my prices I will repay when I am in commissioned work."

"And when will that day come, Tosh? I fear you have been dishonest. What is this remunerative work of which you speak of in the letter? You know that all of these grand London schemes you discuss with Mr Geddes and his ilk always come to nothing."

He took a half-smoked cheroot that had been stubbed in an ashtray and lit it up.

"The Government again, I'm afraid. But the work to which I refer in the letter is more for Mr Bassett-Lowke. . . . advertising posters for his engineering company. I have already started work on them, so you see I do not lie to William. I could never be untrue to him."

No sooner had he lit the cigar than the light bulb filament faded to nothing and they were lost in the dark of a winter's twilight.

"I suppose it's just as well," said Margaret. "Now I can't see the dirt on my cuffs. The landlady never washes anything. I'll soon be slapping the linen on flat stones by the Thames embankment."

She took his matches and lit two candles.

"It's Thursday. Will you go to the Blue Cockatoo tonight?"

"Oh yes," he said. "We both will. Bassett-Lowke's payment is guaranteed so we can have some wine. And Fergusson will be there. He is bringing some canvasses to show me. I can learn a lot from him."

It was a low-roofed, cavernous place and they sat at their favourite table in the gloomiest corner. They did not consider themselves high-profile but had many friends and acquaintances who might even be called famous. They were members of a Labour Party-connected group attempting to bring art to the masses, to foster it in the working class. This group included many painters and also literary figures such as Siegfried Sassoon and Ezra Pound who could often be seen dining there or drinking at the bar. The Mackintoshes were always welcomed at the Blue Cockatoo with open arms and hailed by the other clientele, but often felt embarrassed about it. They may have been short of money but clearly had plenty of goodwill.

A waiter lit their candle and a gypsy violinist began to serenade them. Margaret turned her eyes to the ceiling in frustration when Mackintosh threw the gypsy a sixpence, but she did not chide him. The waiter came back with a bottle of claret and two glasses. Margaret could see it was the expensive stuff and this time she was about to object that they had, as yet, ordered nothing.

The waiter, a middle-aged man with elaborate, Dali-esque moustaches, caught her concern and said quickly in a very fake French accent: "Compliments of Monsieur Fergusson."

He nodded towards a nearby table and they looked over to see the familiar figures of John Duncan Fergusson and his partner, the dancer Margaret Morris, waving at them. Mackintosh beckoned them and asked the waiter to bring two more glasses.

Fergusson was as good as his word and carried three canvasses in a big shoulder sack. At age forty-eight, six years younger than Mackintosh, he was still strikingly handsome, aqualine-featured and clean shaven, and foremost among the Scottish Colourists. This good-natured Leither had lived the dream, had lived in Paris for seven years until the outbreak of the Great War . . . the War which had robbed Mackintosh of so much, of his chance to create at home and his opportunity to move to Vienna. In Paris, Fergusson had lived with the Impressionists and had known Matisse and Picasso. But it was Claude Manet who had left the biggest "impression" on the young Scot. Now though, he had embraced the heavier brush of Fauvism, though his landscapes and portraits, mainly of beautiful women, still reminded Mackintosh of Edgar Degas.

Mackintosh was glad that Margaret Morris was coming to his table and not the other way around, for it give him the chance to watch the way she moved. He had never seen anything like it in any human of either sex. The cliché Poetry In Motion was put to shame by this woman, this living Fairy Queen, this inventor of Celtic Ballet. Her exquisite feet seemed not to touch the ground. Her displacement of the air around her seemed to create ethereal and uplifting music such as might be heard if passing through Heaven. At twenty-two years old, she was twenty-six years Fergusson's junior and would have many love affairs outside of their relationship. Yet she loved him truly and thought him a brilliant and original artist, despite the heavy French influences.

"Drink up my friends, and don't look so guilty. For once I can really afford it."

"Your Chelsea exhibition did well. JD?"

"Aye, and I'm also working for the Royal Navy. Going to Portsmouth to paint battleships. They're getting their own back for not managing to conscript me during the war."

"How ironic for a Colourist to be painting battleships," said Margaret Mackintosh. "Mostly grey, aren't they?

"But surely there will be some green and blue for the sea and sky."

"My dear lady, have you been to Portsmouth? Battleship grey for everything, I'm afraid. Even the people. And you, my dear Toshie. What colour are you tonight?"

"Like Margaret's imagined Portsmouth I think. Blue with cold and green with envy. Don't those sailors down there need some nice, new administrative buildings? Couldn't you recommend me? I could do with a big military commission."

Fergusson drained his first glass of claret.

"Defence budget's shot to pieces, if you'll pardon the pun. No money for buildings. New building equals nissen hut . . . even for the top brass. Anyway, I thought you were concentrating on watercolours these days. Scotland needs another great painter. I'm fed up flying the Saltire on my own."

Mackintosh, despite being more than thirty years her senior, never failed to bring out the mothering instinct in Margaret Morris.

She said: "I should think it is very hard to concentrate on anything, John, when one is hungry, eh, Charles? Look at Margaret, she's as thin as one of her dreaming women, and you are so very pale yourself, Charles, my dear."

She called for menus.

"I know those digs you call home are cold and damp and that your studio is unheated. I hope you do not take us to be intruding, my dears, but we are not here by accident tonight. Tonight you will be our guests, but first JD has a proposition for you. I like to think that we have become such close friends and we do care about you so."

Fergusson had a totally captive audience.

"Look here," he began. "We're getting out of this horrid English winter and we want you both to come with us. Middle of next month we're off to the South of France, to my wee house in Collioure. We want you to come and have a holiday. But listen, it could turn out to be so much more than a holiday for you. You could go and live there. I have many friends there and could give you letters of introduction, which I feel you will scarcely need. And you could both live so cheaply there . . . for much less than what these thieves are stealing from you for those London hovels. It is just the place for you, Tosh,

141

if you are serious about your new painting career, and the climate will do wonders for your health and constitution."

Margaret's reaction was kneejerk.

"The South of France is for the idle rich, John. We couldn't afford one night in Cannes, Nice or Monte Carlo."

"No, no, my dear," said Margaret Morris. "The Pyrenees . . . . Port Vendre, Collioure, Ill-Sur-Tet, Montpelier, Mount Louis. That region is a quiet paradise. At Ill-Sur-Tet there is a gorgeous little hotel, Hotel Fleur, where you could live for four shillings a day and where the food is good and plentiful. The people are simple and kind and it is altogether the ideal place for a few months of rest and work. You could do good work there, both of you. It could be a whole new lease on life for you, and John and me could visit you, if we may."

For half a minute no one spoke. All thoughts danced on the gypsy's violin. But the young dance queen began to see faint smiles creep across the faces of two of the three surviving members of The Four.

Suddenly it became clear to Mackintosh that this is what they were going to do. He was not drunk and his mind was clear. It began to seem like destiny. His career as an architect was over. He had won nothing since Derngate. Now he would be a painter. And where better to be a painter than in France? He could sell his work there and they still had Margaret's allowance. And Wiiliam Davidson would send him the money he had asked for and keep buying from him. He always did.

CHAPTER TWENTY

Destiny

He sat by his easel in a bright yellow field on a gloriously sunny and warm day in February. Their short holiday with Fergusson and Morris had ended but it was only the Colourist and his dance queen who had gone back to London. The Mackintoshes had stayed. It was 1927 and they were now in their fourth year in the South of France. The years had been happy, if not prosperous, but he now had more than eighty paintings completed and was working towards a London exhibition. Fergusson was still a regular visitor and had all the contacts.

At age fifty-nine, Mackintosh had gone through another mini-metamorphosis. Four years of good food and wine had given him a much fuller figure and his face had been tanned by the year-round sun. His hair had thinned even more and was now almost white-blond. He coughed a lot, and hobbled on his bad leg, so his countenance was that of an old man. His cough, of course, was not the result of any cold and damp, but of his chain-smoking. But he was content. His French, if not good, had become more than workable.

He painted his watercolour, pipe dangling from his lips, watched by the beautiful twin daughters of Pierre Dugarry, the farmer who let him use this field. They were called Estelle and Marianne, ten years old, their hair as yellow as the field but cut short in a boyish bob. Dugarry, a widower, preferred it that way. The twins were all he had to remind him of his beloved late wife and he thought that short hair would give them a better chance of avoiding accidents. . . . like the one with the thresher machine which had killed Hortense seven years earlier. Dugarry blamed himself and he always would, simply for the fact that he hadn't been present.

"Picasso has been here," said Estelle.

"And Gaugin, and his friend Vincent, the crazy Dutchman," chimed in Marianne.

He seldom became lonely in the fields but was nevertheless pleased to have their company.

"You are very precocious madmouselles," he said. "You know about art?"

Estelle wasn't sure what precocious meant but was far too proud to ask him.

"No, we don't know about art, just about the people who come here to paint. We talk to them. They are all crazy. Are you crazy too?"

"Well, I suppose I must be, since I am also here."

They were amused by this reply.

Marianne said: "I will not marry a crazy artist."

"Well then will you marry a sane one?"

"I will not marry at all. I will be a nun at the convent of Saint Theresa."

"A bloodless bride of Jesus," he said. "Ah, what a waste."

At this, they turned and skipped away. They had never before met a blasphemer before. Mackintosh watched them melt into the field, moved by their innocence and by the incredible beauty surrounding him, experiencing the kind of appreciation for this Eden that could only be felt by someone who was born and raised in Glasgow.

There was a subtle change in the light as the sun started to sink behind Dugarry's massive barn. He began to clean his brushes.

They had moved to the Hotel Du Commerce at Port Vendres after their first year. The owner, Jacques Dejean, allowed them cheap bed and half-board. He was glad to have them. He thought they were a good advertisement, especially for the restaurant. They always sat at the same table, near the terrace window overlooking the sea. Dejean placed an opened bottle of wine on their table every night. Whether they'd ordered it or not it was always there waiting for them. He had never charged them for a drop. Now Mackintosh poured her a glass, but only a half-glass for himself.

"I always feared I'd lose you to drink, Tosh, but now you hardly touch a drop. Monsieur Dejean could be forgiven for feeling insulted, you know. The wine is excellent."

It was a downbeat opening, delivered in a gloomy voice. Most unlike her.

"I always felt my drinking to be a symptom," he said. "A symptom of something that does not exist here in France. But if only I could get a decent smoke . . ."

Something caught in his throat.. He hobbled out on to the terrace and spat in his handkerchief. He returned coughing.

"Blast this French tobacco, It makes my tongue burn so. . . "

She had given up trying to tell him that he could always quit. Painting, for him, went hand-in-hand with either chomping on a lit stogie or sucking on a fully going pipe.

"Forgive me Margaret," he said, resuming his seat. "I see no reproach in your eyes, but only sadness, your expression so solemn."

"I was thinking of Frances," she said. "How she would have loved it here. And of Sylvan. We have so little word from him from South Africa. "

"Poor Herbert," he said. "He lives on alone in Glasgow, a shadow of the man he was. I am finding it hard to forgive him for destroying all her work. Everything she had in storage and at their flat. But I can see how such intense grief could make a man behave like that. But to deny Sylvan anything to remember her by . . . "

"MacNair thought Frances died of a broken heart," she said. "But it was breast cancer. She'd been hiding it from him for years. You know, Tosh, some people believe disease to be hereditary."

She stood up and walked out to the terrace to gaze at the shimmering white line the moon had drawn across the black water. She came back and, reaching across to him, took both his hands in hers.

"We have been happy here, Tosh, these four years. Wrapped up in each other in all this warmth and light and glory. Dejean says he has never known a more loving couple which, from a Frenchman, is really something. Like teenage newlyweds, he says, or Romeo and Juliet. He displays your work for sale to the hotel guests. He buys your paintings himself. He criticises them only to the extent that there are no people in them. I told him that is because we don't need anyone else . . . but I was wrong . . . "

She took her hands from his and began to softly weep.

"There is someone else I need, Tosh. A doctor. I should not be drinking wine lest it aggravates my pelvic pain. My endometriosis has become worse this past year. I fear it could be something worse. I must return to London for treatment. I have opened correspondence with Doctor Bruce at the Westminster Hospital. He advises that I should not delay."

He had crumpled, crestfallen, into his chair. She knew what he was going to say so she quickly continued.

"There can be no question of you going with me. You must stay here and finish your work if you are to have your exhibition. I don't want you to come to see me during my treatment. I must insist on this, Tosh. I have insurance to meet the cost. Jessie Newbery offered me London accommodation but I plan to stay at the hospital until the treatment is over. I will return as soon as I am satisfied that I am in no danger."

He raised his bowed head to reveal heavy tears.

"But Margaret, we have never been apart."

****

He was back in his favourite spot in the yellow field, putting finishing touches to one of his pastoral studies. Still no people. He couldn't have borne it. She had been gone two weeks and he was quite wretched. It was very hot for March and he sat jacketless in a big wide straw hat, shirt sleeves rolled up, puffing on the ever-present cheroot. But he found that he could not keep the small cigar between his lips as he painted. It was burning his tongue. In fact, his tongue felt so odd, so sore, that he felt he must examine it. He took a small vanity mirror given to him by Margaret which he used for various painting purposes and stuck out his tongue as far as he could, The discolouration alarmed him. His tongue was almost entirely black.

He set down his brushes and picked up his pen, using his sketch pad to write her a letter.

"My Darling. I hope your treatment is going well. M. Dejean had prepared a good dinner for me last night. One dish would have pleased you -- fried jambon and broad beans. I dined quite alone and they have the happy idea to give me still a full bottle of wine and I have the good and happy idea to drink only about half of it. The day has been perfect. Bright sun and not a breath of wind, so I had a good morning's work. Nothing could be more perfect than sitting where I was this morning, only you did not come to meet me and that was a great sadness. Nobody has arrived yet to stay at the hotel, but there were two people at lunch so I was not quite alone. It seems queer to have your room opposite empty ---- very queer and very lonely. I don't think I have ever spent such a long, lonely time and I hope you will never need to go away for so long again".

He put the letter carefully in his folder and sat gazing into space. What should he do about his tongue and sore throat? Of late, he had not been enjoying his smoking. He couldn't afford a doctor, especially here in France. He was distracted from his reverie by an acrid smell. Had he properly stubbed out his cigar? Yes, there it lay, crushed underfoot. But the smell persisted, a smell that did not belong here in this fragrant field. It was certainly the smell of smoke, but not the kind of smoke that comes from a cigar. It was the smell of heavy, black smoke, the kind that comes when buildings burn and paint blisters. He turned around and saw that it was coming from the barn. Even at this distance of some four hundred yards, he could see little winks of red flame through the big open shutters on the upper level. His first thought was to get to the farmhouse and raise the alarm, but if there were anyone there they must already know about it since the farmhouse was but a hundred yards from the barn. He would go to the village and alert the fire tender. He made off in that direction, abandoning his easel and rucksack. But the village was two miles away and he suddenly realised with a strange conviction that if he went there it would be too late. He turned on his heel and made for the farmhouse as fast as his bad leg would allow.

He had a lifelong terror of out-of-control fire, but he seemed to be acting independently of himself. He hadn't a clue what he would do when he reached the barn. He told himself that by the time he got there they would probably have the blaze under control. . . Dugarry and that big man-mountain labourer of his. They would probably be leading out the horses first.

But as he drew near, he saw that the blaze had taken hold with a vengeance and that some beams and sections of roof had already collapsed. It was an inferno and the barn was going to be destroyed, but he saw with great relief that a number of horses had managed to get out and were now careering, terrified, around the yard.

Suddenly, a blackened figure emerged from the slip-door, in convulsions of coughing and weeping. It was Madame Le Brun, Dugarry's mother who had come to stay with them after the death of Hortense. Well into her sixties now, but she made good speed as she ran towards him and prostrated herself at his knees.

"The twins," she cried. "Estelle and Marianne. I cannot find them anywhere. Last night they slept in the barn to be with their sick pony. They went back in after breakfast today. Help me, please M'seiu. . ."

He was close enough now so that the heat from the blaze was making him sweat. He knew there was nothing on earth that would make him enter that outhouse.

"Where is your son?" he shouted to her "And his worker?"

"They left for Perpignan early this morning. The market. Please, we must hurry."

Her words made him feel sick at heart . . . and nauseous. He was sure he was going to throw up. But then something very strange happened, something which he would later consider to have been almost miraculous, though he did not believe in miracles and had always scoffed at the claims of the Catholic Church regarding the appearance in 1858 of the Virgin Mary at Massabielle, three hundred miles to the west. Yet here it was, another miracle in a country of miracles. He suddenly became possessed of a surety and a coolness that seemed to settle on him like the Holy Spirit. Pausing only to ask exactly where the twins would make their beds, he ran for the slip door and entered the blazing inferno.

He was fortunate in that the blaze had started far to the left of the slip-door and that the main conflagration centred there. The roof at that point had collapsed and charred rafters were open to the sky. He heard sobbing from above. Where was the blasted ladder? There was no time. What were there names again? For a moment he could not remember. Then it came to him. The one who said she was going to be a nun.

He called out "Marianne, Marianne"
The girl's face appeared over the railing above him.
"You must jump. Jump now, quickly. Do not be afraid. I will catch you."
He steeled himself and prayed that his bad leg would hold.

Outside in the yard, the grandmother's weeping had turned to wailing. He was taking too long. But then the slip-door burst open and she saw Mackintosh stagger though it carrying one of the twins. The child's face was black and she seemed to be in a fit of uncontrollable sobbing but otherwise she appeared unharmed. Mackintosh fell on to his hands and knees and retched into the dirt. His throat burned, His tongue felt four times its normal size. He got up and ran back for the slip-door with the gait of a man in a three-legged race.

Madame Le Brun comforted her grandchild and waited. The entire upper level of the barn was now ablaze and the section of roof still erect was just seconds away from collapsing. This time, the little Scottishman did not re-emerge. Madame Le Brun knelt in the dirt. She prayed.

And then it happened. The entire edifice came crashing down in a great mushrooming pall of smoke and flame and falling timbers. Madame Le Brun clung to her grand-daughter and began to moan as they gaped at what must surely have become the fiery tomb of little Estelle and Le Petite Ecosse. She hung her head and wept. But when she lifted her eyes it was to see Marianne running and pointing. There, on the other side, where the farm track began to descend towards the sea-gate . . . a man crawling, and beside him the supine figure of her twin sister. They skirted the site of burning devastation and ran to the stricken pair. Estelle lay inert and her white smock was stained with blood. Mackinosh was frantically brushing burning embers from his hair and clothing. He was bleeding from a long cut along the side of his right hand. Alarmed by the sight of the blood on

149

the motionless little girl, the grandmother thought she must be dead. She bent over her grand-daughter, looking for signs of life, shouting the girl's name.

Mackintosh moved to comfort the woman, his voice a near-inaudible croak.

"Don't take on so," he gasped. "The blood is mine. She's going to be all right."

CHAPTER TWENTY-ONE

Return

At long last he was finding out what it was like to be treated like a celebrity and he wasn't sure he much cared for it. Propped up on big pillows in his bed at the Hotel du Commerce, he wondered who would be next in through the door. In the past few days the line of visitors had seemed endless. The twins had both made a full recovery and exaggerated tales of his amazing courage were spreading throughout the district. His room was filled by flowers and gifts. Dugarry had come in every day, beside himself with shame and self-recrimination, pledging eternal gratitude, offering anything in return. He told Dugarry that the best way to repay him would be hush the whole thing up. Dejean, meanwhile, would take no more money for his bed and board, affording him the status of a national hero. He wondered how long that would last.

The local press had been and gone. He would not see them. Now he was steeling himself for a visit from the reporters from Marseilles.

He still didn't know how he could have forced himself to twice go into that burning barn. Perhaps that was all his life had been for. . . everything in it leading him to that particular place at that particular time, his sole purpose under the universe to be there for those children in their time of life-threatening peril. To save them. If so, he decided, that was okay by him. What did all the rest of it really matter when it came to saving the lives of those two beautiful innocents, to banish their terror. He felt somewhat redeemed.

There was yet another knock at the door and Dejean stuck his head around the jamb.

"Forgive me, msieu," said. "Ihlee is here, asking for you. I told him to go away, that you need rest. But he won't take no for an answer. I think he wants to bask in your light."

There was a scuffling outside the door and in barged Rudolph Ihlee, the little bald-headed English artist who lived at Coullioure. Ihlee had married a Frenchwoman and gone native, which gave Dejean the perfect excuse to tease him at every opportunity. Ihlee and Mackintosh had spent several evenings together, smoking and discussing the new art movements of cubism and surrealism that were taking Europe by storm.

"Out of my way, peasant."

Ihlee pushed past the hotel owner and into the room.

"Don't you know never to keep a great man waiting. My friend, he needs me."

Dejean lost no time in joining with the banter.

"The great man is not waiting, it is I who is waiting on him. Certainly it cannot be yourself to whom you refer. The only thing you are great at is running up your bar bill and leaving me unpaid. And don't bother offering me another painting. Thirty-two of your floral studies are quite enough for one hotel."

Ihlee was hot for the duel.

"Bah, philistine. When I am hanging in The Salon those floral studies will make you a millionaire. Out of my way."

Dejean would have liked nothing more than to stay and continue the verbal sparring, but duty called. He took his leave with a final shot.

"You are more likely to be hanging from a gibbet than in The Salon."

Ihlee closed the door on his opponent and sat on the edge of the bed.

"So now you are a hero, my friend. I have come to share your happiness. You are a marvel, Mackintosh. You never seem to get depressed and now you are a local celebrity."

Mackintosh took a flask and two shot glasses from his bedside drawer and poured two generous whiskies. He lit a small cigar, which immediately triggered a violent coughing fit. Ihlee looked concerned.

"It's only a façade, Ihlee. I am much more depressed than anyone could imagine. You say that you drink with me because you are prone to brooding about lack of money and that I cheer you up. But believe me my friend, your deepest depression is something equivalent to me not being very well. I keep my deepest depressions to myself, whereas you constantly exhibit your own, like a child. It works for you and makes you an object of sympathy. A display of my dark emotions would only frighten people."

"You're missing Margaret more than you thought you ever would, eh?"

"No, Ihlee. I knew exactly how much I would miss her. The pain that I anticipated has arrived at exactly the right weight. This is optimum suffering. A numbness sets in. A man refuses to rise, or to feed himself. The happy accident of my convalescence means that, for now, I don't have to do these things. Mt friend DEjean takes care of me. But I tell you now, Ihlee, that were it not for Margaret I would have no desire to recover . . . no desire to walk abroad in the world again."

"Mon Dieu. What it must be to love a woman so."

He could not stay bedridden for long. Two days after Ihlee's visit saw him back among his easel and paints, down on the shore, painting some rock formations.

The village children came. They sat on the sand in little groups, watching him. It was too much of a distraction so he put down his brushes and lit a small cigar. One of the bigger boys produced a cigarette of his own and dared to ask Mackintosh for a light. He decided to lecture the boy on the dangers of a disgusting habit, to show him his discoloured tongue even, but then he realised he would be struggling with his inadequate French. And then he saw her.

She was dressed all in white and had taken off her sandals as she walked along the shoreline towards him. His heart leapt when she removed her straw hat to reveal the auburn hair. He began to run, in that strange gait of his, out to the headland, towards her.

Dejean had kept her room for her, next to his, and now he helped her to unpack. Her treatment had gone well. She had, she told him decided only yesterday to come back early. She had wired from

Calais. He had not received it. He did not care. He was just ecstatic that they were together again. She had heard from Dejean all about his heroics in saving the little girls. She told him that he always been her hero.

That night he called for a celebration and they dined at their favourite table near the terrace. It was a beautiful evening. They spoke of the future. He told her they should be looking at a joint exhibition in London, not just one for his work. He had drunk a lot of wine but she stayed in his room and they slept in each other's arms. But in the morning, when she awoke, she found him lying unconscious, half out of the bed with his head on the floor, the floor itself near his table covered in thick, viscous blood vomit.

****

In a private room at the Westminster Hospital, a group of white-coated medical students crowded around the only bed. The bed contained a patient, but this occupant did not recline the conventional position. Here there were no propped up pillows, no grapes, no chocolates. Instead, Mackintosh was down on all fours, facing the foot of the bed where hung his progress chart. His head was clamped in a cage-like contraption, for support. His tongue was out, extended grotesquely to an unnatural length, held at the tip by a small plastic vice. The whole bizarre apparatus looked like something from a torture chamber and this analogy was endorsed by the state of the horribly elongated tongue, which showed all mottled black and grey.

The students were not taking notes. They all held sketchpads and were drawing the tongue. Mackintosh, despite being unable to speak to them, either nodded or rolled his eyes when they presented their studies for his examination.

In an adjacent office, Margaret sat with Margaret Morris, Fra Newbery and Dr Robert Simpson, surgeon and member of the board.

154

"I understand that any further delay could kill him, doctor. It is already almost a month since we returned from France. The lumps on his tongue must be cut out now, the whole tongue if necessary, to save his throat."

Simpson was a man of good integrity, unselfish and dedicated. There was not a pompous bone in his body. But he looked sad.

"I agree completely," he said. I would operate today but my hand is stayed by the administration. The kind of care that your husband requires will, I fear, be very expensive. In many ways this is a new field for all of us. If you could give an indication of how the costs will be met, I could . . ."

Margaret Morris, empress of dance, had had enough.

"For God's sake, man, hang the expense. We'll get you the money somehow. Just get to work."

Fra Newbery could see that the surgeon found the question of a payment plan distasteful. He said to him:

"Charles Mackintosh, doctor, has no money. In his entire sad, beautiful and distinguished life he never made a penny to speak of and often lost money for his partners. Yet he remains one of the greatest architects who ever lived and, I believe, he has much more to offer a country which is sinking under a blight of post-modern, utilitarian blandness. The Glasgow School of Art, of which I myself have had the honour of promoting in however small a way, is his masterpiece. But he has enriched that city in so many other ways. The great Anglican Cathedral at Liverpool, for which he was so shamelessly usurped, was also created in the mind and soul of this man. There are, of course doctor, many more fine buildings and feats of interior decoration too numerous to mention here today. But the point, doctor, is that I believe there are many more to come. We must save this man for what he still has to offer."

CHAPTER TWENTY-TWO

Ashes

He had outlived his usefulness as a medical guinea pig. The students had enough drawings of his tongue. It was cancer and it had spread to his throat.

He told her he didn't want to spend Christmas in a hospital. There was no need for him to be there anyway. His radium treatment required him to be only a once-a-week out- patient.

She rented the house in Willow Road where he liked to sit under the tree in the garden. When he came out of the hospital he couldn't speak at all. Margaret Morris gave him voice exercises but it was too painful and he soon resorted solely to sign language. Later that year, they moved to a friend's house in Paddington but in November he went into a nursing home. He died there on December 10. He was sixty years and six months old.

In the spring of 1929, Margaret went back to Port Vendres, but this time accompanied by Fra Newbery and his daughter Mary, the little girl who, thirty years earlier, had stood shivering with a golden key on a silk pillow on the day Mackintosh had boycotted the opening of the art school's first phase. But Mary was 36 years old now and on the grand tour of Europe with her father. However, before the delights of Paris and Rome they had a solemn task to perform here on the Cote Vermeille.

The three of them walked through the village towards the small harbour on another bright, sunny day enlivened by a fresh sea breeze.

"We had seven comparatively happy years here," said Margaret. "I feel as though his spirit is here. He did so much love to come down to the port to practise his terrible French on the fishermen."

"What will you do now, Margaret," asked Newbery. "We could let you have the cottage in Suffolk if you like. We use it so rarely now."

"Dear Francis, always taking care of me . . . of us both. Thank-you, my good, true friend, but there can be only one course open to me and I think you may have already guessed what that is. I shall stay here, of course, where Tosh is, by his side, where I have always been. You don't imagine that I am going to allow a little thing like his death to come between us, do you?"

She turned and walked away from the Newberys, toward the rocky promonitory beyond the harbour where Mackintosh had been fond of setting up his easel. She carried with her a small urn which held some of her late husband's ashes, the rest having been interred at the Golders Green crematorium in London. As Mary Newbery watched Margaret cast the ashes downwind and out to sea, her eyes became moist with tears.

"She is wrong, father," said Mary. "His spirit is not here, but in Glasgow. It never left. God forgive me, but I hope his ghost is there too. And I hope it haunts them."

****

Mary Newbery lived to be 93 years old. She died In Edinburgh in 1985. During the last year of her life, she was interviewed by the writer and journalist Alistair Moffat for a TV programme about Mackintosh. This is what she told him:

They turned against Mackintosh. In 1910, they said he was out of date but time was to prove them wrong. In 1914, just before the Great War, I was taken to Vienna to see some houses by Hoffmann. But Hoffmann had reverted almost entirely to Classical lines. He said to me 'Of course, I was influenced by Mackintosh when I was younger, but that was many years ago'. How fickle and forgetful.

Just a few years ago, at an exhibition in London, it interested me that what they had made in Vienna in Mackintosh's day was still being cherished --- the Cabbage Dome, the Bank, the Old People's Home, the Hoffmann furniture ---- all of which the guide, an Austrian, said could not have been done without the influence of Mackintosh. It was galling that, while all of these Viennese buildings were still beautiful and in use, the Mackintosh stuff in Glasgow was in a terrible state.

One of Mackintosh's prettiest buildings is the Scotland Street School. Well, now everything around it has been pulled down and a motorway goes past it. There are no children left there to go to the school. It has two staircases locked in glass baronial towers and Mackintosh's love of children is evident in it. The cloakrooms have hot pipes above and big hooks standing out where any wet coats hung there for a few hours will be dry when the children are ready to go home. Few architects would have bothered. The Queens Cross Church now also has a motorway running past it and, of course, they've pulled down his beautiful building in Ingram Street which the Corporation was due to buy but never wanted.

I suppose it's just another sad sign of these sad times. In Mackintosh's day, Glasgow was a vibrant place, but now all the rich people --- the rich people with style, anyway ---- have gone away. I remember Mrs Cargill, that's Burmah Oil, in a chinchilla coat arriving at the St Andrews Hall and being saluted in the most dignified way by the rather exciting Russian conductor Milnarski. Do you think that sort of thing happens now? I imagine that the people who own Burmah Oil probably live in the Bahamas now. They certainly don't live in Glasgow. You need rich people . . . people spending money, buying pictures, getting houses built. But, of course, they didn't get houses built by Mackintosh, as one might have hoped.

After the second phase of the School of Art opened, Mackintosh didn't get much work, partly because Glasgow was too provincial. They thought the tearooms were a joke and the School of Art very peculiar. The reason why Mackintosh left Glasgow was very simple. He broke his partnership with Keppie. They never really got on. There was the thing with Jessie and I think there may have been some ill-will. After he left Keppie, nothing came his way. He went in for quite a lot of competitions but you could spend your life doing that and losing. He didn't get Liverpool Cathedral and when he didn't get the Dough School it might have reinforced the notion that he was being deliberately excluded. He told me about this himself. He said they had turned down his plans because the wash-hand basins were on the wrong side of the corridor. One of the judges told

158

me later that Mackintosh's designs were infinitely better than anyone else's. He said that a thing like that, the basins, would simply be altered after the plans were accepted. A simple adjustment. And so Mackintosh realised that if they wouldn't accept his good plan, then they were putting him off with an excuse. I think it was that that made his give up on Glasgow.

People have often asked me if there was an unseen hand behind the rejection of Mackintosh . . . some pernicious force determined to batter him down each time he showed such promising signs of a meteoric rise. I think that the answer must be yes although, of course, nothing can be proved. He spent the second half of his life in deep hatred of Charles Reilly, the Liverpool professor who had voted on the Cathedral competition, though I was never quite sure why and he would never let on. I only know the facts, and the facts are these. Sir James Burnet, the man who built the extension to the British Museum and the most powerful architect in Scotland in Mackintosh's day, was later to show his true colours. Perhaps he thought that no one would notice but, after the Great War, Burnet --- a man who had been very anti-Mackintosh, couldn't bear him ---- blatantly copied him. Burnet took great chunks of House For An Art Lover and made very pretty houses using the external detail.

Looking back now, I feel terribly, terribly sad at the waste. Here we have this brilliant man whom it would pay you to use and he wasn't given any real use at all. Of course, if he'd got Liverpool Cathedral, the Dough School or those studios in London, he could have gone on to greater things because, by the end of the Second World War, other architects were using his ideas. Thinking back now, the tears come to my eyes and I feel so sad that the genius was wasted. I feel great sadness when I hear of these high prices. I think how happy the Mackintoshes would have been with just a hundredth part of that money. I have a lot of pleasant, friendly memories of Mackintosh, but I could weep at the waste of his genius.

There exists another interview given to a reporter by Desmond Chapman-Huston, the author and poet, who had befriended the architect both in his Glasgow and London days. It is remarkable in how much it mirrors the testimony of Mary Newbery.

It was the School of Art, you know ---- his masterpiece. He never really recovered from his daily fight for nearly five years with the Corporation Committee responsible for the funding of it. It was a continuous heart-breaking struggle that finally broke him. Glasgow has, for its municipal buildings, one of the most boring and mediocre of late Victorian concoctions and the Glasgow people really have nothing to look at in a city which has, since then, been no more than an ugly slum. Yet the Glasgow people like to pretend that they discovered Mackintosh, employed him and made him famous. They did no such thing. So little did they think of his potential that they gave him for his masterpiece a steep, cramped site on a hillside in a narrow back street. From no angle can the building be looked at or its significant form, magnificent proportions and fine detail and craftsmanship be examined. Glasgow's banal City Hall, pompous, derivative university --- even its cinemas --- all received worthy sites. But its one architectural gem ---- the Mackintosh School Of Art --- had to make do with a cheap and sordid setting.

In those days there was in Glasgow a fine and notable woman, a Miss Cranston, who bult up a very successful tea-room business. Uneducated, but cultured, it was she --- a private person ---- who first recognised and employed Mackintosh. She gave him the best available sites and a free hand and he made her three unique restaurants. My favourite was the Willow Tea-rooms in Sauchiehall Street. He designed the building and every piece of furniture in it, even the teaspoons, while Margaret, whose decorative creativity complemented his own, did all the decorations. He was fond of saying in his love for her "Margaret has genius, I have only talent" but I do not think that this was true. Margaret's art was derivative and heavily influenced. Toshie's was masterfully original and fluid ---- and he still had that gift even after he became disillusioned by years of neglect.

The houses he built are magnificent pieces in their own right, but they were also beloved homes to the distinguished people who commissioned them. He declared that no architect could make a home for anyone he did not know well . . . nor should he even build a house unless he had a voice in choosing the site, the garden and the

160

furniture. This is what they couldn't stomach. So many people who wanted to employ him, but did not because they found him too demanding. They could not see that this was his dedication.

Employing only the finest available craftsmen, accepting only the finest materials and workmanship and never hurrying, he lost money on every job he undertook, was the despair of his partners and lived --- and died --- a gloriously poor man.

The cathedral at Liverpool would have made him, you know. And his entry for it was brilliant . . . a clear winner. But they wouldn't let him have it, of course, although they were not above stealing from his design. The winner of that competition had, of course, been decided even before the competition was advertised. Such a travesty that it had to be Giles Gilbert-Scott, grandson of the great George Gilbert-Scott, the man who built the empire. Clearly, this was a nod of deferment to the great man, who had recently passed on, for young Giles was, how shall I put it, somewhat limited in his abilities. Poor Giles was an absolute wizard at designing anything as long as it required no more than four sides, a base and a lid. It is no accident that he is principally known for two of the most iconoclastic boxes in Britain . . . Battersea Power Station and the Red Telephone Booth. They had to prop up young Giles's cathedral design by borrowing heavily from Mackintosh's entry.

After the Liverpool rejection, Mackintosh began to drift. But he revolutionised world architecture. Acclaimed in Europe while he was ignored at home, much of what has since passed in English architecture as "modern" is merely Mackintosh and water.

EPILOGUE

A Room With A View

Not long after he left the firm, he had begun to work from home at the house in Florentine Gardens. He couldn't afford too keep on the Scott Street office, nomatter how dingy it was. Margaret suggested that, even with no office, he would still need a secretary. He supposed she was right, so she placed an advertisement for him.

One of the respondents was a young man, distinguished from the others not only by his youth and his gender but by his cultured English accent and perfect diction. His name was Desmond Chapman- Huston and he would befriend Mackintosh until death. He would later in his life become successful himself and even take it upon himself to organise Mackintosh's funeral.

But on this particularly dank and dreich early evening in Hillhead, in the summer of 1913, it was a somewhat impoverished-looking young man who found himself in the Florentine Gardens drawing room. Chapman-Huston did his best to dress like a gentleman but Mackintosh saw that his coat sleeves were frayed and his shirt discoloured. There was a small hole in the toe of his left boot. Despite this, he had a stately bearing, clear eyes, good teeth, a direct, honest manner and a pleasant voice.

Mackintosh, who considered himself a good judge of character, liked what he saw straight away, but the obvious question was how such a young man came to find himself in Glasgow.

Chapman-Huston explained that he had come up from London with his father, ostensibly to look after the old man. Arthur Chapman-Huston was a penniless and alcoholic actor whose wife had died when Desmond was a child. Arthur had travelled north with a touring company now staging a play at one of the big Glasgow theatres ---- something by Sheridan and not very well attended. Arthur had a small part and it would no doubt be a short run.

162

Desmond himself was working at the theatre as a dresser for his father but for no money. The old man did not keep well and Desmond knew the old man depended on him.

"Good of you to see me first thing, Mr Mackintosh," he said, as his host offered him a chair. He sat down and pulled over his coat flap to hid the frayed knee of his trousers.

"First thing, indeed," said Mackintosh. "Is it first thing? Yes, I suppose it must be, if you say so. I'm afraid the accepted structure of a day as perceived by most people means very little to me. Oh, but please don't let that put you off. I would never expect you to be on duty at the crazy times when I work."

The young man was in no way fazed. "Not at all, sir. I think you would find me a most flexible employee, ready and willing to serve when required and not merely within the confines of a pre-determined shift."

"You are then, not a married man," hazarded Mackintosh.

"No, sir. There is only myself and my father . . . an actor, you know. His name is Arthur. He calls himself Arthur King, if you can believe that. He is fond of reciting the whole of the Tennyson poem and possibly believes himself to be the reincarnation of one of the Knights of the Round Table, probably the gallant Sir Galahad. You won't have heard of him, my father I mean. At the moment he is touring with Sheridan's The Rivals. I am dressing for him but soon the season will close and we have nothing else lined up except the long journey back to London, where I should think we will have to busk."

"You appear to be an educated man, Mr Chapman-Huston, but would my employing you not interfere with your theatre work?"

The young man suppressed a bitter smile. "What I do at the theatre could hardly be described as work. I am more of a skivvy really. I run around doing favours for the most obnoxious people. I would be honoured to work for you. I am an admirer. If you will forgive me for saying so, I think it is criminal the way you have been marginalised."

Mackintosh was intrigued. "You are young", he said, "but still you too know what it like to be special and yet ignored. I will be happy to take you on."

"May I ask a favour of you sir," blurted a delighted Chapman-Huston. "Would you show me your house?"

On the other side of the River Clyde and not too far from The Gorbals, Arthur Chapman-Huston, a.k.a. Arthur King, sat huddled around a smoke-choking charcoal-and- sticks fire in slum tenement digs that constituted one room and an outside toilet the Glaswegians called a cludgie. He thought it must be the only word in the English language that rhymed with budgie. Well, he certainly wouldn't have to use it, since his stomach was empty and he was starving. Where the hell was Desmond?

He sat crouched with a woollen shawl wrapped around his shoulders. He couldn't believe how cold it was in this country on an alleged summer's evening. He hated Scotland . . . hated playing to its ignorant masses. He had "died" on stage in Glasgow a hundred times --- and not through any theatrical swordplay. He was trying to concentrate on reading a book. . . . a dog-eared filthy copy of Ibsen's Hedda Gabler. He planned to audition for the part of the Judge once they got back to London ---- back to civilisation. The Ibsen play was sure to have a long run in the West End and he deluded himself that he was perfect for that particular role.

He pulled the shawl closer around himself and took occasional swigs from a green bottle containing the cheapest gin. On his empty stomach, the hard liquor made him feel nauseous, but that would pass. Still, he was bloody hungry too. Desmond had promised to bring back fish and chips. Queer bloody interview, he thought, having to go to a person's house. Something fishy there, but this thought only made him hungrier.

He began to drift into melancholia. The gin always did that to him. But just as he was about to nod off, there was heard footfall on the landing and the sound of a key in the lock. Desmond came in carrying a greasy parcel and gave it to his father. He took off his coat and threw it on the bed, the only place in the room he could have put it short of dumping it on the floor.

164

"Bah, this is cold," said Arthur, "and soggy with vinegar. You know I hate too much vinegar. Where the hell have you been until this time. Not drinking in pubs, that's for sure. Not chatting up chorus girls. Too bloody refined for that sort of manly behaviour aren't we, Desmond?"

Desmond sat on the edge of the bed a looked squarely at his father.

"I'm not going back to London with you, not this time anyway. You can take my share of the train fare. I've taken a position as a private secretary to an architect . . . six months initially, with an option to extend the arrangement if both parties are satisfied. I will be moving into his house."

Arthur grew angry, and fearful. He was afraid of losing the son who worked for him for nothing and yet who was also a potential meal ticket.

"An architect? What architect? Somebody I should have heard of, is it?"

"Mr Charles Rennie Mackintosh, a married man. His wife is something of a designer herself, I understand. But he needs a secretary. I am to be his man."

Arthur spat soggy chips into the grate. "Charles Rennie Whomacktosh? Why, he's not even famous. A nobody. Can he pay you? It won't last long . . . and don't come crawling back to me when he hits hard times and gives you the elbow. An architect, indeed. Anybody can call themselves an architect. Their worth is fleeting. Their prosperity comes and goes. They're only in it for themselves. He'll work you like a dog and then dump you like a dead one. Ruthless types, like lawyers . . ."

Desmond looked around the revolting room and then got up and walked to the single window, careful not to touch the soot-stained rags that served as curtains.

"No father," he said. "You have not seen his house or been in his company. If you had, then you'd know what it's like to be in the presence of true greatness . . . to be cheek-by-jowl with true beauty."

"What are you talking about? Are you in love with him or something?"

165

"You are probably unaware of it, father, but it is a beautiful evening out there. Soft, as he natives call it, and with the dying light having that certain Northern quality. When I left here earlier today I walked westward along that interminably beautiful boulevard called Sauchiehall Street which, I subsequently learned, means Street Of The Willows. Ascending out of a misty valley, I reached my destination and was ushered inside by a neat Scottish maid. The lady of the house was not home, I was informed, but my prospective employer awaited me upstairs. I was in a long, narrow hall, softly lit and covered completely in a rich pile carpet, soft and as rich as the fur on a Siamese cat. The feeling of restful space was extraordinary. Following the maid upstairs to the first floor, I was shown into a large L-shaped room with two fireplaces. It could have been a studio, yet it was not. It may have been a drawing room, but certainly not of the cluttered, overbearing kind that I have known. My host, smoking a small cheroot, rose to greet me and placed me in a large box-armchair, the likes of which I have never seen. He took a similar chair opposite. I was, I instinctively realised, talking to a great man. There is something at once humbling and exhilarating about true greatness of any kind and, moreover, my surroundings were, in the full meaning of the word, unique. The room was a shrine and, to a man like me who has known only an oppressive plethora of Victorian furniture and decoration, the room was an oasis, a revelation, a delight. It was all ivory white, relieved with pieces of dark wood, hand-made furniture and skilfully selected patches of vivid colour. The curtains were carefully designed to keep the windows in the room, but the dominating feature was a splendid window at one end, facing south-west."

Arthur had listened to this monologue with no small enjoyment and fascination. His son had delivered it as if in a rapturous trance, like someone back from the dead who had seen God in His Heaven. Now he screwed his fish-and-chip paper into a ball and threw it on the smouldering fire.

"Bah," he said. "Why would he make a window the dominating feature?"

Desmond turned to look at him.

166

"For his wife Margaret, he told me. So that she could watch the sunsets."

THE END